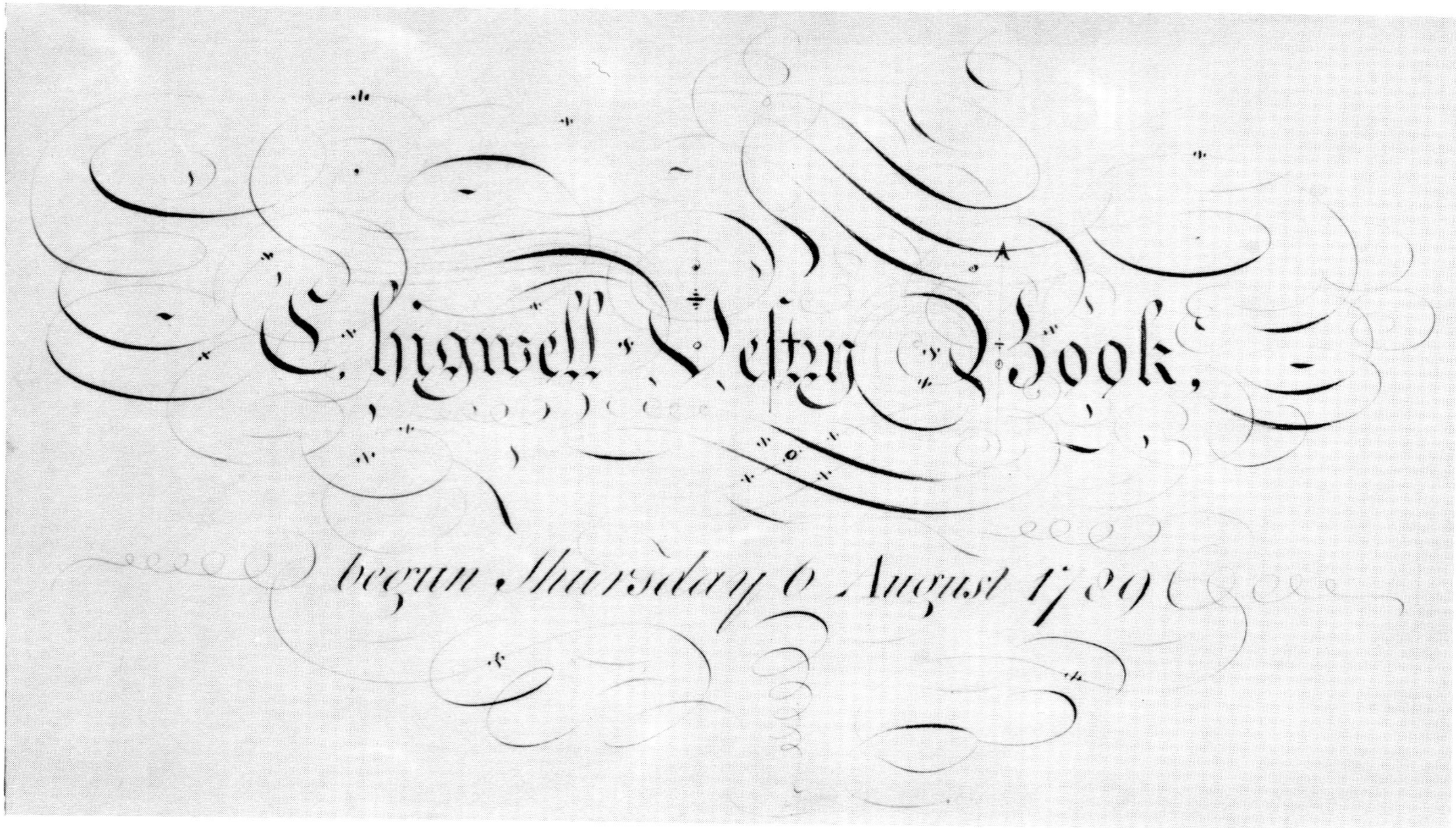

TITLE PAGE OF A VESTRY BOOK

Reduced.

An example of the fine penmanship sometimes found in parish records; written by John Vickery, a master of Archbishop Harsnett's Grammar School at Chigwell.

EXAMPLES
OF
ENGLISH HANDWRITING
1150—1750

With Transcripts and Translations

PART I : FROM ESSEX PARISH RECORDS
PART II : FROM OTHER ESSEX ARCHIVES

By
HILDA E. P. GRIEVE, B.E.M., B.A.,

PUBLISHED BY THE ESSEX EDUCATION COMMITTEE
ESSEX RECORD OFFICE PUBLICATIONS, NO. 21
1954

5th Impression 1981

ISBN 0 900360 31 3

CONTENTS

Title page of Chigwell Vestry Book, 1789		*Frontispiece*
Decorated Initial V from Great Waltham Court Roll, 1541		*Title page*
Foreword		
Secretary Alphabet, 1571		*Fig.* 1

PART I : EXAMPLES FROM ESSEX PARISH RECORDS

	Page	
The Scripts. Notes contributed by R. W. Hunt	i	
The Abbreviations. Notes contributed by N. R. Ker	i	
Grant of Land, Little Waltham, *c.*1275	1	*Plate* I
Title Deed of Charitable Income, Harlow, 1324	2	II
Churchwardens' Accounts, Saffron Walden, 1478	3	III
Churchwardens' Accounts, Great Hallingbury, 1528	4	IV
Churchwardens' Accounts, Great Dunmow, 1540	5	V
From an early 'Parish Book', Great Easton, 1578	6	VI
Churchwardens' Inventory, Chelmsford, 1582	7	VII
Parish Register, Stanford Rivers (transcribed 1582)	8	VIII
Form of Vagrant's Certificate, Stanford Rivers, 1598	9	IX
Parchment Transcript of Heydon Register, 1599	10	X
Constables' Accounts, Woodford, 1649	11	XI
The Sexton's Duties, Waltham Holy Cross, 1658	12	XII
Relief of the Poor, Thaxted, 1703	13	XIII
A 'Hue and Cry', West Tilbury, 1728	14	XIV
Repairing the Ashdon Highways, 1734-5	15	XV
Constables' Accounts, East Ham, 1743	16	XVI
Translations	17	

PART II : EXAMPLES FROM OTHER ESSEX ARCHIVES

Notification of Gift, Mountnessing, *c.*1152	19	XVII
Grant of Land, Fryerning, *c.*1170	20	XVIII
Exchange of Land, Takeley, *c.*1212	21	XIX
Manor Court Roll, Great Waltham, 1318	22	XX
Extract from Manorial Survey, Thaxted, *c.*1395	23	XXI
Extract from Manorial Compotus, Foulness, 1425	24	XXII
Indented Bill of Receipt, Ingatestone, 1543	25	XXIII
Extract from Manorial Survey, Great Baddow, 1605	26	XXIV
Household Accounts, West Horndon, 1612	27	XXV
Enrolled Will, Kirby-le-Soken, 1613	28	XXVI
Deposition taken by Justices of the Peace, 1623	29	XXVII
Extract from Inventory of Goods of Robert, Lord Petre, 1638	30	XXVIII
Translations	31	
Short list of books for detailed study and reference	33	
Alphabets from A. Wright's *Court Hand Restored* (5th ed., 1818)		*Loose inside back cover*

FOREWORD

Part I of this book reprints *More Examples of English Handwriting* (1950). Part II replaces *Some Examples* (1949), mostly by new, full size, examples, with transcripts now uniform in method with those in Part I. That is to say, all transcripts are exact, and for ease of comparison set out line for line as written, the layout following closely that of the MSS. When abbreviation is extended or expanded, the letters omitted by contraction or suspension, or represented by special signs, are supplied in square brackets (e.g. Int' t'ram=Int[er] t[er]ram); when contraction by superscript letters is expanded, the omitted letters are placed in square brackets, the superscript letters are printed in *italics* (e.g. Q^{i}ete=Q[u]*i*ete; o^{r}=o[u]*r*). Any indication of abbreviation when extension or expansion is doubtful or impossible (cf. p.3 n.1) is marked by an apostrophe (e.g. p.4 n.1, p.5 n.1), or by the reproduction of superscript letters (e.g. p.8 n.2; for exceptions to this, see p.2 n.2 and p.8 n.1). ff has been printed F; and capital I standing for I or J, according to modern practice (e.g. John, not Iohn). The reproductions (with the exception of the Frontispiece and Plates XVII, XVIII and XXII) are full size, and have been made from documents in the Essex Record Office.

It is a pleasure to thank those who have given me such friendly and invaluable assistance : Mr. F. G. Emmison, the County Archivist, for constant support and many helpful comments; Dr. R. W. Hunt, Keeper of the Western MSS., Bodleian Library, for contributing the Note on the Scripts in Part I; Mr. Neil Ker, Reader in Palaeography in the University of Oxford, for contributing the Note on the Abbreviations in Part I and for most patient and constructive criticism of the notes on the text in Part I; Miss K. Major, Reader in Diplomatic in the University of Oxford, and Professor F. Wormald, Professor of Palaeography in the University of London, for most useful suggestions; and all my colleagues, and in particular Mr. D. M. Shorrocks, for advice, checking and correction, at every stage of preparation of the book. I am, of course, entirely responsible for all errors that remain.

January, 1954 H.E.P.G.

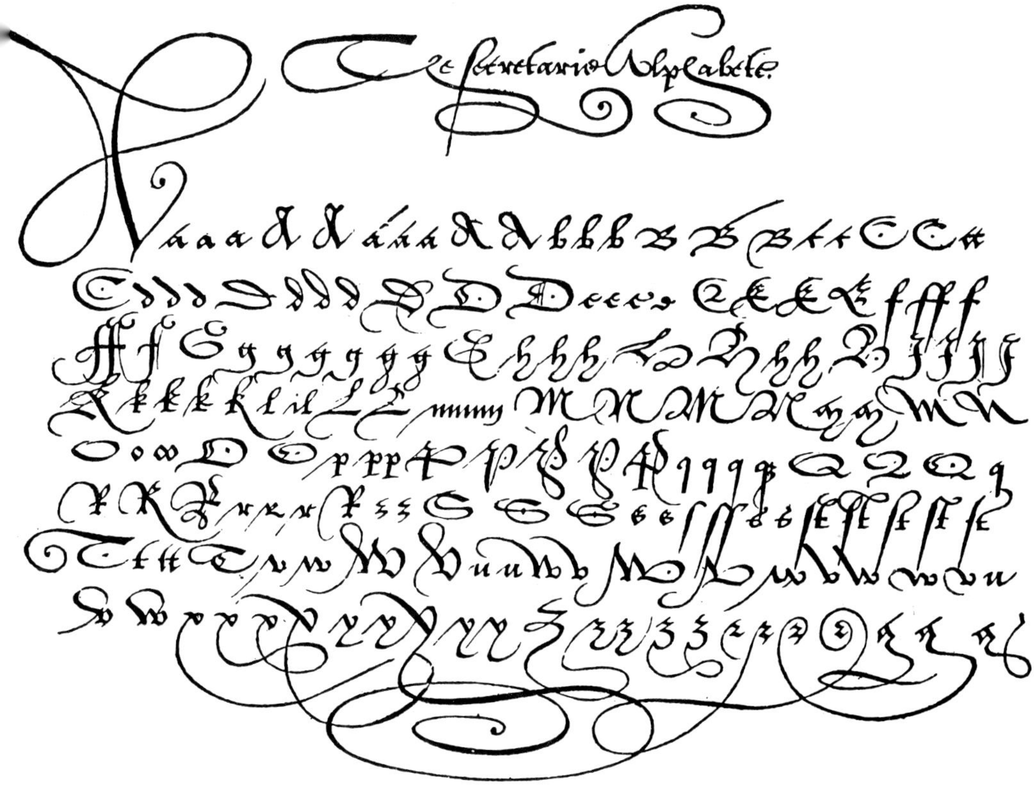

FIG. 1

Secretary Hand, from the first English engraved copybook, *A Booke Containing Divers Sortes of Hands*, by John de Beauchesne and John Baildon, London, 1571. Reproduced by permission of the Trustees of the British Museum.

PART I

EXAMPLES FROM ESSEX PARISH RECORDS

THE SCRIPTS

The plates in this collection, ranging in date from the late thirteenth to the late eighteenth century, show a wide variety of scripts and very different kinds of skill and formality. The two medieval deeds (Plates I and II) are the work of professional scribes with a strict training. Several of the later examples are the work of men to whom writing was a labour, as we should expect in a collection made from parish records. Plates III-V show late medieval or Tudor types of hand. Plate III is interesting as an early dated specimen of this type. In the middle of the sixteenth century a reform was made and henceforth the influence of the writing masters with their engraved specimen books predominates[1]. The Elizabethan type of script is known as the Secretary Hand (Fig. 1 and Plates VI-XII). It continued in use until about the middle of the seventeenth century. The first example (Plate VI) is the work of a not very skilful clerk, the second (Plate VII) is the hand of an educated man writing large and carefully. In Plate IX we have the writing of a man who used both the secretary (in the body of the document) and the italic hand (in the headings). This latter, a modified form of the humanist or Italian hand, came to be used more and more in the seventeenth century and finally displaced secretary. The writing masters of the late seventeenth century developed a new variety of the Italian hand which is the ancestor of copperplate, the chief English contribution to the development of writing in the later period. Plate XIII shows a transitional type of hand in which some of the old letter forms of secretary (e.g., *e* and often *r*) are retained. Plate XIV is an uneducated man's version of the new hand. Plate XV is a variant with legal associations often seen in the first half of the eighteenth century. Plate XVI shows the progress towards copperplate. The Frontispiece is the work of a school master, and is a sample of the flourished penmanship so lovingly cultivated by the writing masters.

R. W. HUNT

THE ABBREVIATIONS

The first two plates show the medieval system of abbreviating Latin manuscripts by contracting and suspending words, an admirably efficient system of shorthand writing, which was easy to master and admitted of little ambiguity. The 17 lines of Plate I include 169 marks of abbreviation, not counting the sign for *et*. The 13 lines of Plate II include 156 marks of abbreviation. In each specimen rather less than half the marks are special signs, each of which has a value or values of its own[2]. The rest, 88 in Plate I and 85 in Plate II are more or less horizontal strokes[3]. All these marks are made according to rule and not according to the whim of the scribe. Indeed to know how to write the letters of the alphabet was only part of a medieval scribe's task. He had to learn also how to shape his marks of abbreviation and how to apply them correctly. Like the rules for making and combining the letters so too the rules

[1] See Ambrose Heal, *The English Writing Masters and their Copy-books*, 1570-1800, Cambridge, 1931, with an important introduction on scripts by Stanley Morison ; A. Fairbank, *A Book of Scripts*, 1949, pp. 16-20.
[2] See p.1, notes 1,3,5-8,10,13; p.2 notes 1,3,4.
[3] See p.1 n.4.

of abbreviation changed slowly from generation to generation. One method of abbreviation seen in Plate I, *c*.1275, had not been long in common use[1], and another seen in Plate II, 1324. is not found commonly before the fourteenth century[2]. The sum total of these changes is considerable, so that the system of abbreviation in use in the fifteenth century differs a good deal from that of the thirteenth. Inevitably mistakes were made in applying the marks of abbreviation[3], but in the thirteenth and fourteenth centuries they are surprisingly few, even in the work of provincial writers. Later the scribes failed often to make the marks correctly and the broken-down system of abbreviation ended by being a nuisance instead of a convenience. It is particularly tiresome as an accompaniment to writing in the vernacular of the fifteenth and sixteenth centuries.

When the scribes wrote in English they used the special signs designed for Latin so far as they could. Some of these signs proved fairly useful in English, e.g., those for *pro, pre, per* or *par*, and the mark showing omission of *er*. One sign, that for final *is*, was adopted to mark the plural in *-is, -es*, or *s*[4]. The horizontal stroke was used, as in Latin, to mark the omission of *m* or *n*, and the omission of *i* in the ending *-cion* or *-tion* (Latin *-cionem, -tionem*). Along with this legitimate use of abbreviation marks we find very commonly in English their misuse in positions where they are either unnecessary or ambiguous. By the late fifteenth century it had become a well established custom in vernacular writing to draw a horizontal stroke through or above the *h* in all words ending in *th, gh, ght, ch*, to draw a similar stroke through every final double *l*, to extend the last stroke of every final *r, m* and *n* in a flourish above the line and to extend the loop of every final *d* in a downwards direction. These curious customs are shown in Plates III-V[5]. Some of the strokes cannot mean anything, for example when they are used with such words as *well, on* and *for*. Others may, or may not, indicate the omission of a letter[6]. We can be certain that the scribes of these documents did not know what the marks meant. In using them they were merely following the tradition of writing in the vernacular, a tradition which goes back to the fourteenth century and was fully established by the fifteenth in the practice of many scribes[7]. This tradition was not discarded until writing was reformed in the reign of Elizabeth.

Plates VI-XV show examples of writing after the reform. Otiose strokes are to be seen in Plate VI only, 1578[8]. Plates VI-X, 1578, 1582, 1598, 1599, show how the medieval marks of abbreviation continued to be used, correctly and also incorrectly[9]. They were still being used for some time after 1600, but did not survive a second reform of script in the middle of the seventeenth century, except in a few technical uses[10] The scribe of Plate XI, 1649, uses no abbreviations. The remaining plates show scripts of 1650 to 1743, in which almost the only method of abbreviation is that by superior letters such as we use now in writing the day of the month. The common modern practice of suspending a word and marking the suspension by means of a dot appears first in lines 4-6 of Plate XIII, 1703.

N. R. KER

[1] See p.1 n.6.
[2] See p.2 n.1.
[3] See p.1 n.12; p.2 notes 6,9.
[4] See p.2 n.1, p.5 n.2, p.7 n.5, p.9 n 3.
[5] The scribe of Pl.V flourished *g* as well as *r* and *n*.
[6] See p.3 notes 1,4, p.4 n.1.
[7] The 14th-century manuscript of Havelok the Dane, Bodleian MS. Laud misc. 108, has occasionally a stroke through final *th* (W.W. Skeat, *Twelve facsimiles of Old English manuscripts*, 1892, pl.vii, col.1, ll.10,17: col.2,l.24).
[8] *accompt'*, l.5; *totall'*, l.14.
[9] For examples of misuse of marks of abbreviation see p.7 n.2, p.8 n.2.
[10] E.g. Pl.XV, l.8, *per day*

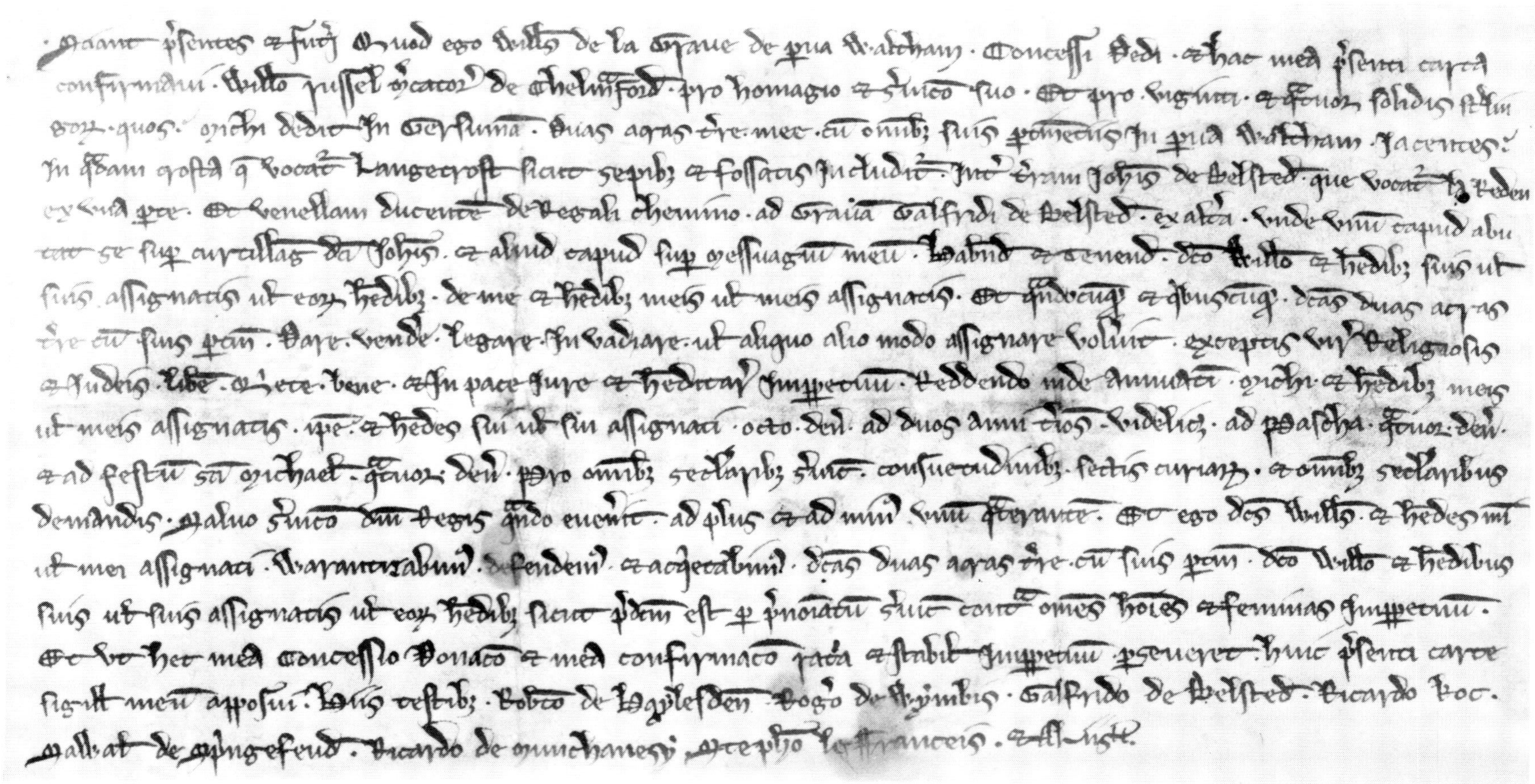

.Sciant p[re]sentes[1] [et][2] fut[ur]j[3] Quod ego Will[elmu]s[4] de la Graue de p[ar]ua[5] Waltham . Concessi Dedi . [et] hac mea p[re]senti carta confirmaui . Will[elm]o russel M[er]cator[i][6] de Chelm*a*[r]ford'[7] . pro homagio [et] s[er]uic[i]o suo . Et pro . viginti . [et] q[u]*a*tuor solidis st[er]lin gor[um][8] . quos;[9] Michi dedit In Gersuma[m] . Duas acras t[er]re . mee . cu[m] om[n]ib[us][10] suis p[er]tine[n]ciis In p[ar]ua Waltham . Iacentes; In q[u]*a*dam crofta q[ue] vocat[ur] Langecroft sicut sepib[us] [et] fossatis Includit[ur] . Int[er] t[er]ram Joh[ann]is de Belsted' . que vocat[ur] la Reden ex vna p[ar]te . Et venellam ducente[m] de Regali chemino . ad Graua[m] Galfridi de Belsted' . ex alt[er]a . vnde vnu[m] capud abu tat se sup[er] curtillag[ium] d[i]c[t]i Joh[ann]is . [et] aliud capud sup[er] Messuagiu[m] meu[m] . Hab[e]nd[um] [et] Tenend[um] . d[i]c[t]o Will[elm]o [et] h[er]edib[us] suis u[e]l suis . assignatis u[e]l eor[um] h[er]edib[us] . de me [et] h[er]edib[us] meis u[e]l meis assignatis . Et q[u]*a*ndocu[m]q[ue] [et] q[u]*i*buscu[m]q[ue][11] . d[i]c[t]as duas acras t[er]re cu[m] suis p[er]tin[enciis] . Dare . vend[er]e . legare . Invadiare . u[el] aliquo alio modo assignare volu[er]it . exceptis vir[is] Religiosis [et] Judeis . lib[er]e . Q[u]*i*ete . bene . [et] In pace Iure [et] h[er]editar[ie] Imp[er]petuu[m] . Reddendo inde annuati[m] . Michi . [et] h[er]edib[us] meis u[e]l meis assignatis . ip[s]e . [et] h[er]edes sui u[e]l sui assignati . octo . den[arios] . ad duos anni t[er][m]i[n]os . videlic[et] . ad Pascha . q[u]*a*tuor . den[arios] . [et] ad festu[m] s[an]c[t]i Michael[is] . q[u]*a*tuor . den[arios] . Pro om[n]ib[us] sec[u]larib[us][12] s[er]uic[iis] . consuetudinib[us] . sectis curiar[um] . [et] om[n]ib[us] sec[u]laribus demandis . Saluo s[er]uic[i]o d[omi]ni Regis q[u]*a*ndo euen[er]it . ad plus [et] ad min[us][13] . vnu[m] q[u]*a*terante[m] . Et ego d[i]c[tu]s Will[elmu]s . [et] h[er]edes m[e]i u[e]l mei assignati . Warantizabim[us] . defendem[us] . [et] acq[u]*i*etabim[us] . d[i]c[t]as duas acras t[er]re . cu[m] suis p[er]tin[enciis] . d[i]c[t]o Will[elm]o [et] h[er]edibus suis u[e]l suis assignatis u[e]l eor[um] h[er]edib[us] sicut p[re]d[i]c[tu]m est p[er] p[re]no[m]i[n]atu[m] s[er]uic[ium] cont[r]*a* om[n]es ho[m]i[n]es [et] feminas Imp[er]petuu[m] . Et vt hec mea Concessio Donac[i]o [et] mea confirmac[i]o rata [et] stabil[is] Imp[er]petuu[m] . p[er]seueret . huic p[re]senti carte sigill[um] meu[m] apposui . Hiis testib[us] . Rob[er]to de Haylesden' . Rog[er]o de Wymbis . Galfrido de Belsted' . Ricardo Koc. Sawal' de Sp[r]*i*ngefeud' . Ricardo de Munchanesy . Steph[an]o le Franceis . [et] aliis .

*Translation on p.*17.

[1] *Note the special sign denoting omission of* re *in the combination* pre- (*cf. n.*6).

[2] *Note special sign for* et. *It was used in English for* and. *For some other forms see p.*8 *l.*7, *p.*14 *l.*3, *p.*15 *l.*2.

[3] *Note special sign denoting omission of* ur. *This particular example is currently written. There are several variant forms of this sign, as e.g.* vocat[ur], *l.*4, *and* fut[ur]is, *p.*19 *n.*2.

[4] *Note the common mark of abbreviation, a more or less horizontal stroke used to mark the omission of the letter* m *after a vowel* (cu[m], *l.*3), *or of* n, *if the* n *is covered by another consonant* (pertine[n]ciis, *l.*3), *and to denote all contractions (as here) and suspensions* (Tenend[um], *l.*6) *for which no special sign is used (cf. notes* 1,3,5-8,10,13; *p.*2 *notes* 1,3,4). *The stroke is sometimes a good deal curved* (porc[i]ones, *p.*2 *l.*3, terra[m] *and* q[ue], *p.*22 *l.*4), *especially at the end of the Middle Ages and later.*

[5] *Note the horizontal stroke through the descender of* p *denoting* per (p[er]tinenciis, *l.*3) *or* par (*as here*). *In Latin literary texts the correct expansion is seldom in doubt, but the use of this sign in names of persons and places is a source of confusion; thus p.*2 *l.*3 *either* p[er]rys *or* p[ar]rys *can be read and p.*2 *l.*4 *the expansion* p[er]ndon *rather than* p[ar]ndon *is assured only by the etymology (see P. H. Reaney,* Place-Names of Essex, 1935, *p.*48). *For its use in English see p.*6 *l.*3, *p.*8 *l.*5.

[6] *Note the special sign denoting omission of* er, *always used, except in the combination* per (*see n.*5), *and after* b, h, *and* l, *when the common mark of abbreviation is used* (h[er]edibus, *l.*6), *and after* s, *when a curving stroke is drawn back through the shaft of the* s (*cf. p.*4 *n.*7). *About the middle of the 13th century this special sign tends to replace the horizontal stroke as a sign of suspension after certain letters, e.g.* r (*as here and* vir[is], *l.*8) *and* n (den[arios], *l.*11; *cf.* p[er]tin[enciis], *l.*8). *It saved the scribe's time by allowing him to make the mark of abbreviation without raising his pen. Cf. n.*1 *for another restricted meaning of this sign.*

[7] *Note the superior* a, *an archaic 'open'* a, *descended ultimately from Roman cursive, closed by a horizontal stroke. This sign is used in the combination* q[u]a (*l.*4) *and when* ra *is preceded by a consonant* (p[r]ati, *p.*2 *l.*4). *There was a tendency from about the middle of the 13th century to make use of it in any combination in which the letter* a *occurred (as here apparently) and to use it also as a mere space saver, without any abbreviation being involved (p.*2 *n.*2). *For its use in the 16th century see p.*3 *n.*4 *and p.*7 *n.*2.

[8] *Note the special sign used with the 2-shaped* r, *a form of* r *used originally only after* o, *but, from the 12th century, after* a *also and later after other letters. The sign commonly denotes* um, *but it is sometimes used as a general suspension, for example in the well-known forms* Sar[isburiensis] *and* Ebor[acensis].

[9] *The inverted semicolon has been printed as a semicolon.*

[10] *The special sign seen here is used at the end of words to denote omission of* us *in the combination* -bus, *omission of* ue *in the enclitic* -que (quandocumq[ue], *l.*7; *the pronoun* que *is abbreviated by means of the horizontal stroke), and omission of* et (videlic[et], *l.*10.) *Originally like a semicolon it came by currency to resemble an open figure* 3.

[11] *Note superior* i. *It is used in the combination* q[u]i *and when* ri *is preceded by a consonant* (Sp[r]ingefeud', *l.*17). *It tends to develop a marked slope from left to right and a rising introductory stroke, and in the end looks more like a French circumflex accent than an* i.

[12] *Here and again at the end of the line the scribe makes an unusual mark to denote the omission of* u *before* l. *The common form here is a horizontal stroke through the* l.

[13] *Note special sign denoting omission of* us, *except after* b (*cf. n.*10). *Its formation is seen more clearly in the three examples in l.*13.

GRANT OF LAND, LITTLE WALTHAM, *circa* 1275

The earliest of 139 deeds found in the parish chest. Although the property was not granted for charitable purposes until 1375, earlier deeds were preserved to prove the title. The names of witnesses give an approximate date.

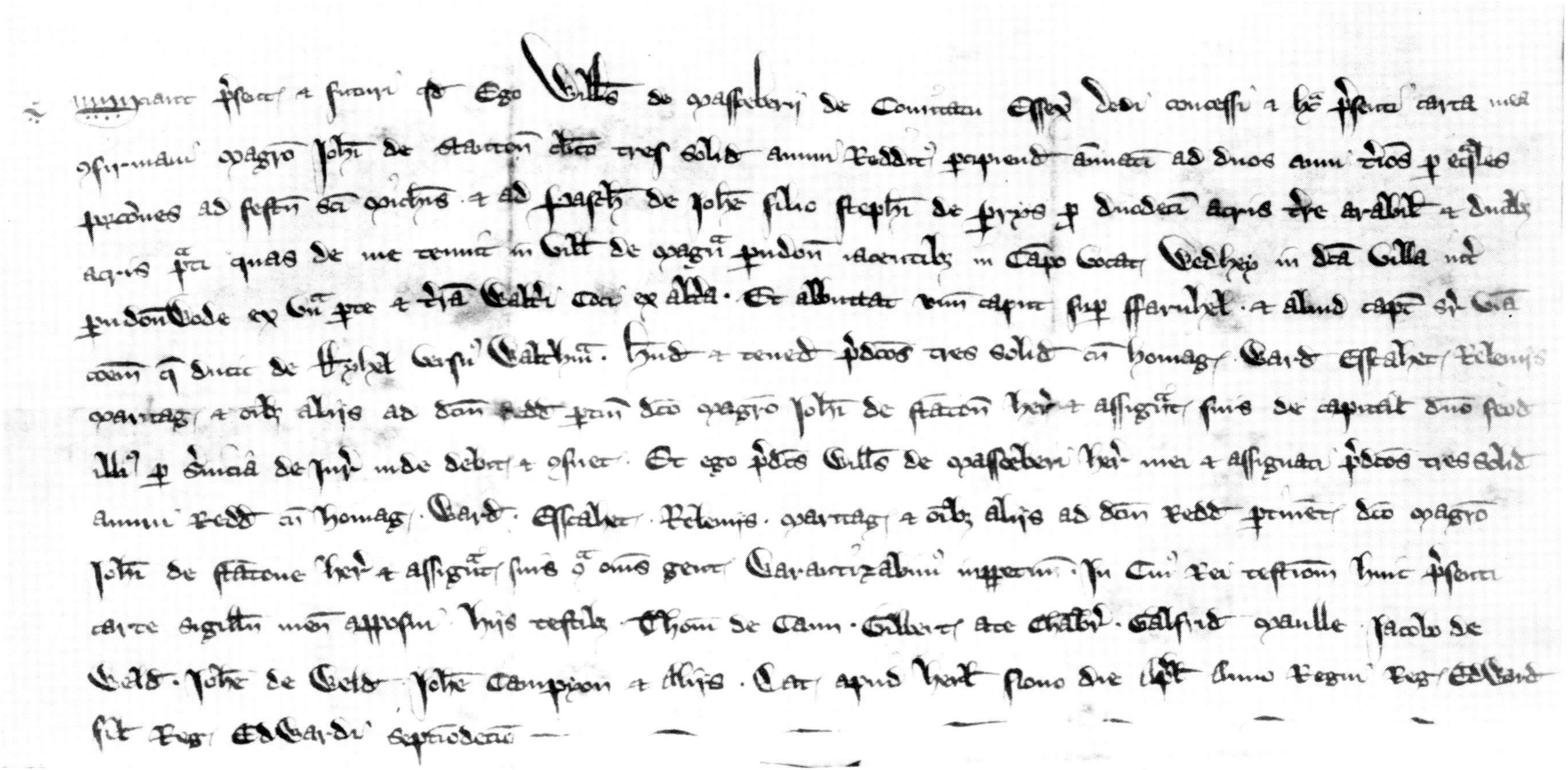

Sciant p[re]sent[es][1] [et] futuri q[uo]d Ego Will[elmu]s de Massceberij de Comitatu Essex' dedi concessi [et] h*ac*[2] p[re]senti carta mea [con]firmaui[3] Mag[ist]ro Joh[ann]i de Stanton[e] cl[er]ico tres solid[os] annui Reddit[us] p[er]cipiend[os] a[n]nuati[m] ad duos anni t[er][m]i[n]os p[er] eq[u]*a*les porc[i]ones ad festu[m] s[an]c[t]i Mich[ael]is . [et] ad Pasch[a] de Joh[ann]e filio steph[an]i de p[er]rys p[ro][4] duodeci[m] acris t[er]re arabil[is] [et] duab[us] acris p[r]*a*ti quas de me tenuit in vill[a] de Magn*a* p[er]ndon' iacentib[us] in Ca[m]po vocat[o] Wedhey in d[i]c[t]a villa int[er] p[er]ndon' Wode ex vn*a* p[ar]te [et] t[er]ra[m] Walt[er]i Coci ex alt[er]a . Et abbuttat vnu[m] caput sup[er] Farnhel . [et] aliud cap[u]t s[upe]r[5] via[m] co[mmun]em q[ue] ducit de Ryhel versu[us][6] Walth*a*m. H[abe]nd[um] [et] tene[n]d[um] p[re]d[i]c[t]os tres solid[os] cu[m] homag[iis] . Ward[is] Esscahet[is] Releuijs Maritag[iis] [et] o[mn]ib[us] alijs ad d[i]c[tu]m Redd[itum] p[er]tin[entibus] d[i]c[t]o Mag[ist]ro Joh[ann]i de sta[n]ton[e] her[edibus] [et] assign*a*t[is] suis de capital[i] d[omi]no feod[i] illi[us] p[er] s[er]uicia de Iur[e] inde debit[a] [et] [con]suet[a]. Et ego p[re]d[i]c[tu]s Will[elmu]s de Massceberi her[edes] mei [et] assignati p[re]d[i]c[t]os tres solid[os] annui Redd[itus] cu[m] homag[iis] . Ward[is] . Esscahet[is] . Releuijs . Maritag[iis] [et] o[mn]ib[us] alijs ad d[i]c[tu]m Redd[itum] p[er]tine[n]t[ibus] d[i]c[t]o Mag[ist]ro Joh[ann]i de sta[n]tone her[edibus] [et] assign*a*t[is] suis [con][tr]*a*[7] om[ne]s gent[es] Warantizabim[us] inp[er]petuu[m]. In Cui[us] Rei testi[m]o[niu]m huic p[re]senti carte sigillu[m] meu[m] apposui. hijs testib[us]. Thom[a] de Cann[8] . Gilbert[o] ate Cha[m]br' . Galfrid[o] Maulle . Jacobo de Weld' . Joh[ann]e de Weld' . Joh[ann]e Campyon [et] Alijs. Dat' apud herl' Nono die Ap[ri]l[is][9] Anno Regni Reg[is] Edward[i] fil[ii] Reg[is] Edwardi septi[m]odeci[m]o ——— ——— ——— ——— ——— ——— ———

Translation on p.17.

[1] *Note suspension after final* g *and* t *marked by a vertical looped stroke attached to the horizontal termination of the* g *and* t; *see also* vocat[o], *l.4*, Reg[is], *l.13. This special sign is not used in Plate XVI and is rare before* c.1300. *Later it ceased to be used as a general suspension and was confined to denoting omission of* is. *For its use in English see p.5 n.2, p.7* n.5, *p.8 l.1, p.9 n.3, p.15 n.1.*

[2] *Cf. p.1 n.7. Other examples of this use of* a *are* Magna, *l.4, and* vna, *l.5. For examples of its misuse later see p.3 n.4, p.7 n.2.*

[3] *Note special sign representing* con. *Originally it resembled a reversed* c. *See also n.7.*

[4] *Note abbreviation of* pro. *For its use in English see* p[ro]vided, *p.9 l.8.*

[5] *Note that the sign used to mark a suspension after the letter* r (*see p.1 n.6*) *is here used in just the same manner to mark a contraction. This time-saving practice of attaching the sign of contraction to the last letter of the contracted word, instead of writing a horizontal stroke separately, came into use in the middle of the* 13*th century.*

[6] *The* u *written here is superfluous; the special sign* (*see p.1 n.13*) *itself represents* us.

[7] *Note abbreviation of* [con][tr]a *by combination of special sign* (*see n.3 above*) *and superscript* a (*see p.1 n.7*).

[8] *This might be* Caun; *the name occurs in the same group of deeds as* Cavnne.

[9] *If the scribe intended the normal spelling* Aprilis *he should have made the sign noticed above, p.1 n.11. The sign he has actually made should strictly be expanded* Ap[re]l[is] (*cf. p.1 n.1*).

TITLE DEED OF CHARITABLE INCOME, HARLOW, 1324

John de Stanton, rector of Harlow, acquired certain lands and rent-charges to endow the Chantry of St. Petronilla in the parish church. Twenty four other fourteenth century deeds, several dealing with the chantry, were found at Harlow.

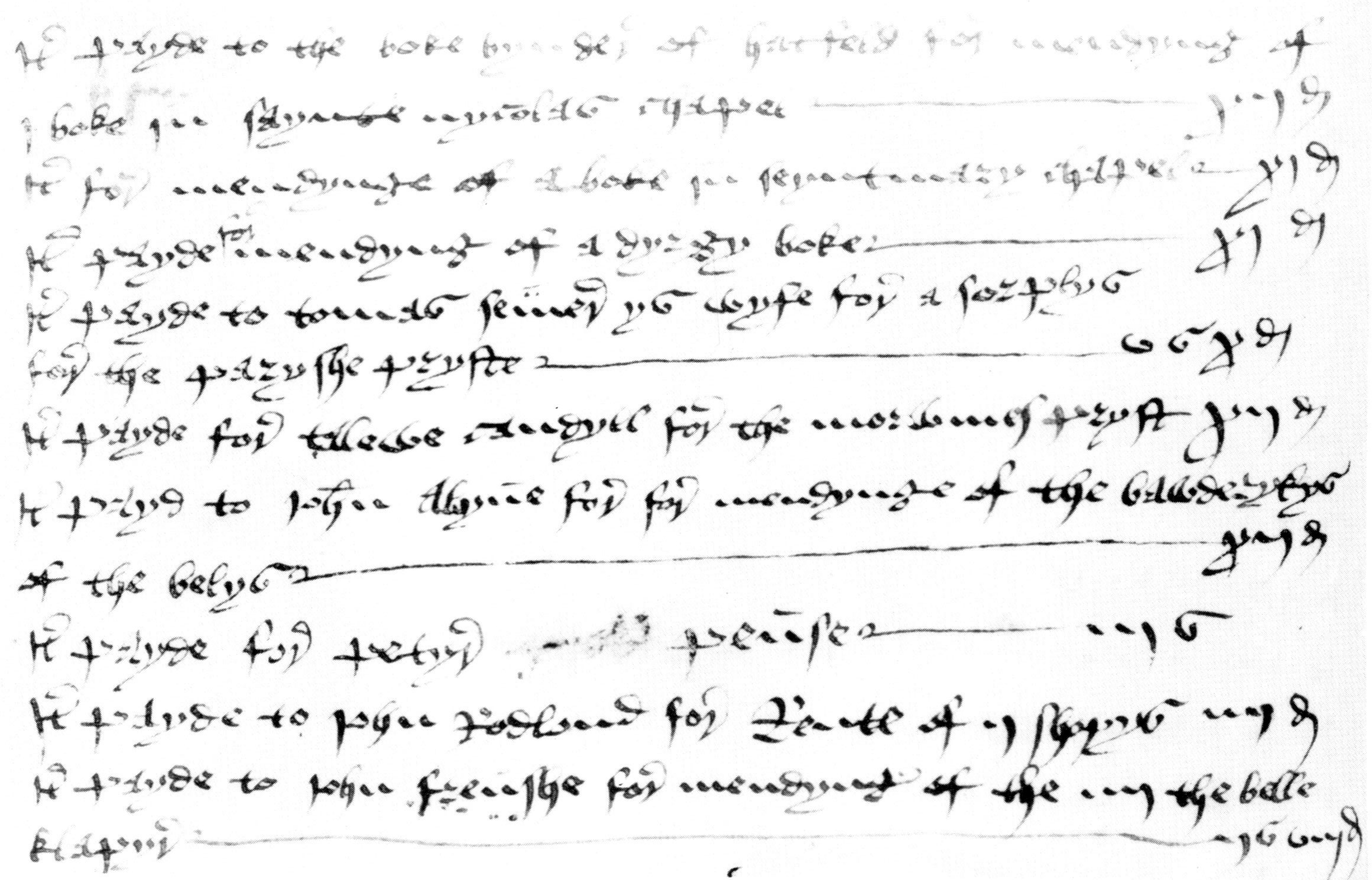

It[em] payde to the boke bynder'[1] of hatfeld for' mendyng of
j boke jn saynte nycolas chapel ——————————— xij d'[2]
It[em] for' mendynge of a boke jn' seyntmary chapel———xj d'
It[em] payde for'[3] mendyng of a dyrgy boke —————xj d'
It[em] payde to tomas sem'er'[4] ys wyfe for' a sorplys
for' the paryshe pryste ——————————— v s[5] x d'
It[em] payde for' talewe candyll for' the morwmes pryst xij d'
It[em] payd to Joh'n[6] Alyn'e for' for'[7] mendynge of the bawderykys
of the belys ———————————————————xij d'
It[em] payde for' petyr'[8] pen'se ——————— iij s
It[em] payde to John Rodlond for' Rente of ij shopys iiij d'
It[em] payde to John frenshe for' mendyng of the iiijthe belle
klapyr' ————————————————————— ij s viij d'

[1] *This writer consistently added a flourish, similar to his suspension sign (see* It[em], *same line) to* r *in the final position. The use of such flourishes and marks of abbreviation (particularly after final consonants, but also generally), not necessarily indicating any specific omission, was common as English gradually superseded Latin (see p.ii). The practice was probably a survival of the convenient habit of suspending Latin terminations. It may also suggest that at a time when English spelling was not standardised some writers were uncertain whether they had properly completed a word. As these flourishes may indicate no more than habit or doubt, in the absence of evidence elsewhere in the same writer's work to justify any particular extension, it is often wise not to attempt it. The flourishes are reproduced by apostrophes.*

[2] *i.e.* d[enarii] (pence). *Note use of Roman numerals* [12d.].

[3] for *interlined.*

[4] *The superscript* a *over* semer *is unusual. This writer frequently, though not invariably, put an abbreviation sign directly over the letters* m *and* n. *He used indiscriminately a superscript* a *or a straight dash (see* jn', *l.3,* Alyn'e, *l.8, and* pen'se, *l.10). This suggests that he regarded the superscript* a *as a general mark of abbreviation; he often used it over final* m *and* n *where it would be more usual to find one of the flourishes described in n.1. The only consistency in his practice was that no letters were affected except* m *and* n. *This is an example of individual habit in the use of abbreviation marks. See also p.7 n.2. The abbreviation marks are reproduced by apostrophes.*

[5] *i.e.* s[olidi] (shillings). *The sum is* 5s. 10d.

[6] *Note the writer's inconsistency; there is no abbreviation stroke over* John *in ll.* 11, 12. *This stroke of abbreviation in the word* Joh'n *is common in the 15th and 16th centuries (see also p.4 l.2) and is clearly a survival from Latin practice, in which* Joh'nes *stood for* Joh[an]nes.

[7] for' *repeated.*

[8] *An erasure between* petyr' *and* pen'se.

CHURCHWARDENS' ACCOUNTS, SAFFRON WALDEN, 1478

Part of a page in one of the oldest surviving parish account books in the country. Most of the entries are in Latin, although Norman-French was used from 1439 to 1441, and later churchwardens occasionally wrote in English. The 'dyrgy boke' was the Office for the Dead; the 'morwmes pryst' performed the morrowmass, or first mass of the day; payment of 'petyr pense' (Peter's Pence) to the Pope, was suppressed by Henry VIII in 1534.

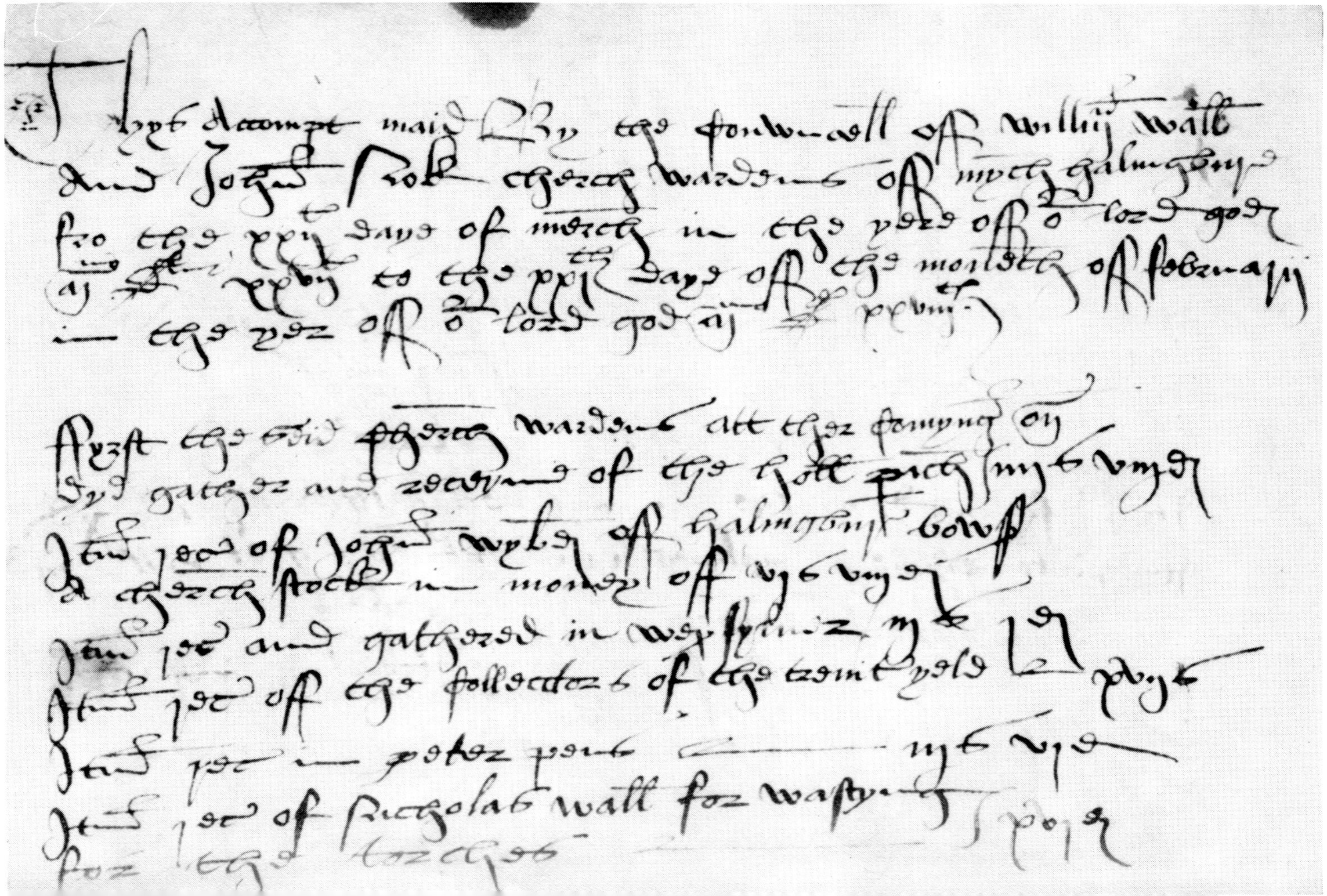

Thys Accompt maid By the Couwncell'[1] off[2] Will[i]*a*m Wall'
And John' Nok cherch wardens off mych' halingbure
fro the xxij$^{t'}$ daye of merch' in the yere off o[u]*r* lord god'
M[^{illesi}]^{mo} DC[^{entesimo}] xxvij$^{t'}$[3] to the xxjth[4] daye off the moneth' off februarij
in the yer off o[u]*r* lord god M[^{illesi}]^{mo} DC[^{entesimo}] xxviijth[5].

Fyrst the seid Cherch' Wardens att ther Comyng' on'
dyd gather and receyue of the holl' p[ar]ich' } iiij s viij d'
It[e]m rec'[6] of John' Wyb[er]d' off halingbur' bows[er][7]
A cherch' stock in money off vj s viij d'
It[e]m rec' and gathered in wex syluer/iij s j d'
It[e]m rec' off the Collectors of the trenit' yeld[8]—xvij s
It[e]m rec' in peter pens——————iij s vj d'
It[e]m rec' of Nicholas Wall' for Wastyng
for the torches———————————— } xvj d'

[1] *Note the free use of abbreviation strokes throughout (see p.3 n.1). Where there is no adequate reason for extension, they are reproduced by apostrophes.*
[2] *Note inconsistency of spelling. The writer uses both* of *and* off.
[3] *i.e.* one thousand, five hundred, and seven and twentieth, 1527. *It is not clear which letters of* Centesimo *are actually written.*
[4] *i.e.* one and twentieth.
[5] *i.e.* 1528.

[6] *As the form* receyue *occurs in l.7, this could be extended* rec[eyued]; *the writer might not however have been consistent (see n.2).*
[7] *Note abbreviation of* ser *(see p.1 n.6)*.
[8] *i.e.* trinity gild; yeld *is derived from the Anglo-Saxon form and modern* gild *from the Norse form of the same word. In many documents the voiced palatal spirant as in* yeld *is represented not by* y *but by the letter known as* 'yogh'. *This letter, descended from the flat-headed Anglo-Saxon* g, *resembles a written* z *(see p.23 n.2) and survives today, for example, in the Scottish name* Menzies.

CHURCHWARDENS' ACCOUNTS, GREAT HALLINGBURY, 1528

Illustrates the varied sources of churchwardens' income before the Reformation.

4

PLATE V

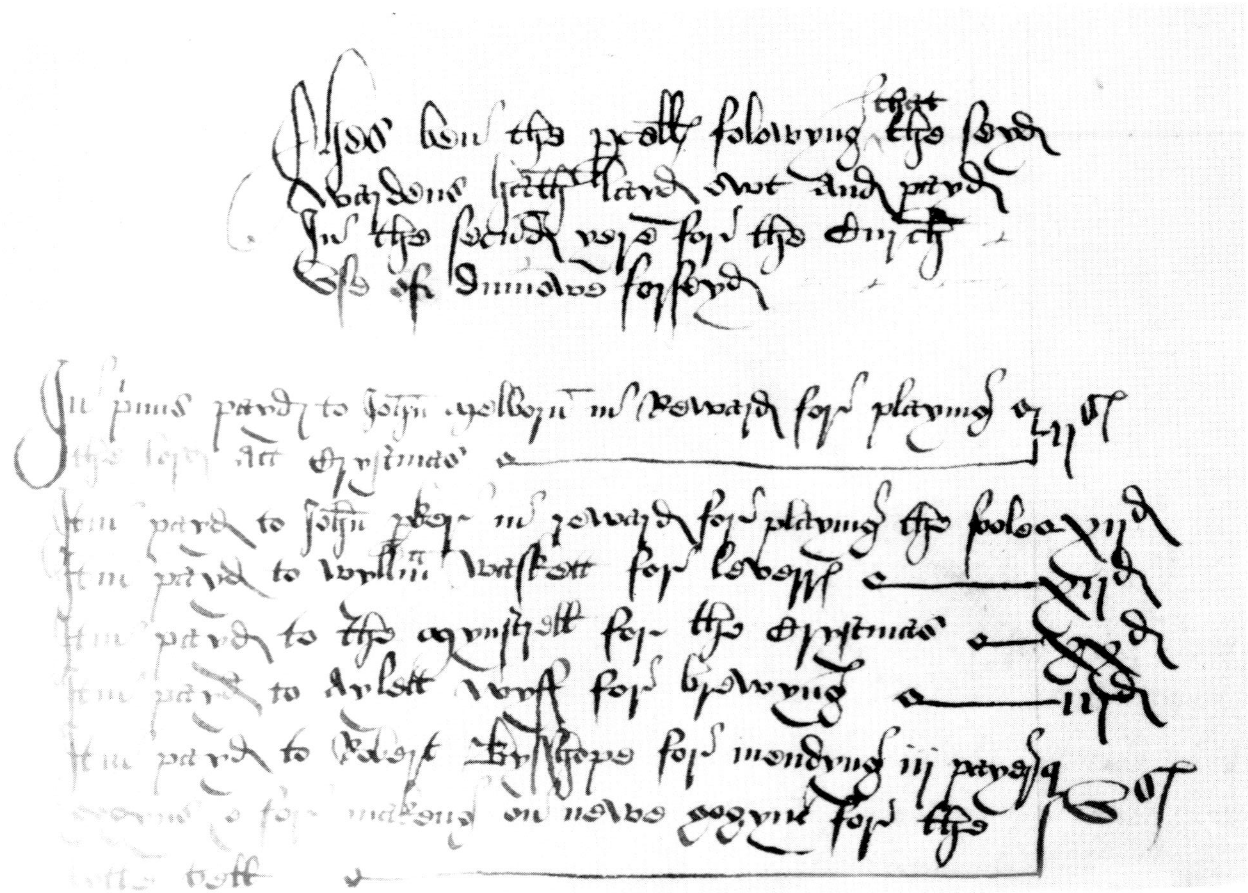

Thes ben'[1] the p[ar]cell[es][2] folowyng' that[3] the seyd'
Wardens hath' layd' owt and' payd'
In' the secu[n]d' yere for' the Curch'
Vse of' Du[n]mowe forseyd'

In' p[r]*i*mis payd' to John' Melborn' in' Reward' for' playing' the lord' att Crystmas	ij^{s}'
It[e]m payd' to John' p[ar]ker' in' reward' for' playing' the foole	xij^{d}'
It[e]m payd' to Wyll[y]*am*[4] Waskett for' leverr[es]	xij^{d}'
It[e]m payd' to the Mynstrell' for' the Crystmas	xx^{d}'
It[e]m payd' to Aylett wyff for' brewyng'	iij^{d}'
It[e]m payd' to Robert Bysshope for' mendyng' iij payer' gogyns & for' makeng' on' newe gogyne for' the lytle bell'	v^{s}'

[1] *The use of final flourishes is very free in this example. They are reproduced by apostrophes.*

[2] *For this looped stroke see p.2 n.1. It has been transcribed* es (*see also* leverr[es], *l.8*) *rather than* s *because the writer elsewhere in these accounts spelt many words which he gave in full with final* e *and* es (*e.g.* pathes, paynes) *and frequently used it when it could have no other meaning* (*e.g.* wag[es]).

[3] that *interlined*.

[4] *This might in fact be either* Wyllam *or* Wyll[y]am. *Though this writer invariably abbreviated the name, in the same accounts another contemporary writer who gave the name in full used alternatively* Wylyem *and* Wyllem.

CHURCHWARDENS' ACCOUNTS, GREAT DUNMOW, 1540

These accounts include many other entries relating to festival plays. As elsewhere, maintenance of the bells was an ever-recurring item of expense.

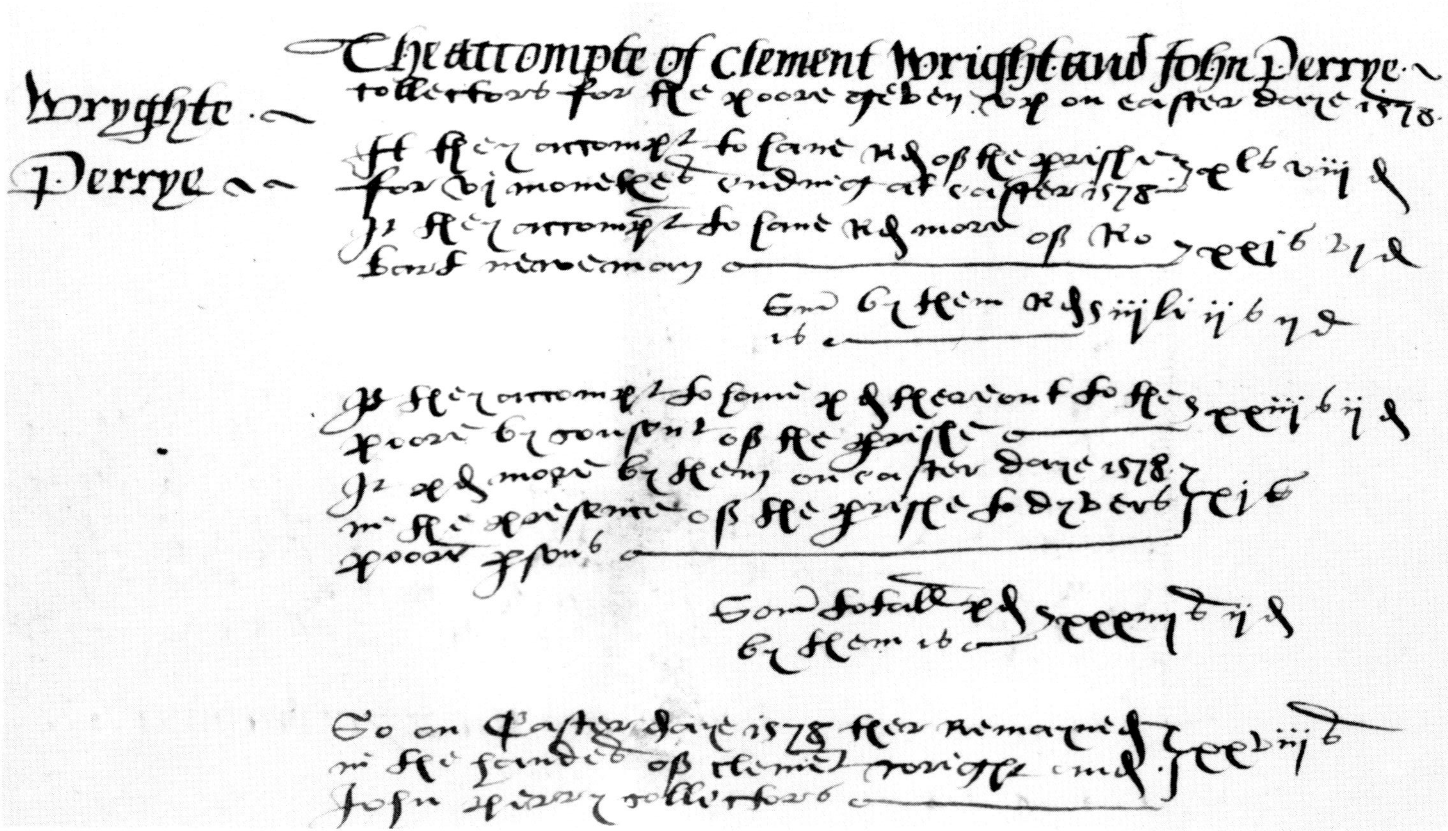

Wryghte

Perrye

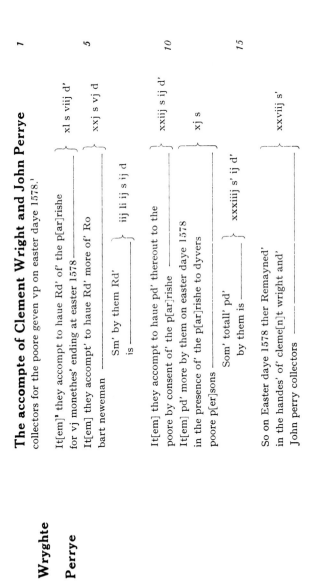

The accompte of Clement Wright and John Perrye

collectors for the poore geven vp on easter daye 1578.[1]

It[em][2] they accompt to haue Rd' of' the p[ar]rishe for vj monethes' ending at easter 1578	xl s viij d'
It[em] they accompt' to haue Rd' more of' Robart neweman	xxj s vj d
Sm' by them Rd' is	iij li ij s ij d
It[em] they accompt to haue pd' thereout to the poore by consent of' the p[ar]rishe	xxiij s ij d'
It[em] pd' more by them on easter daye 1578 in the presence of' the p[ar]rishe to dyvers poore p[er]sons	xj s
Som' totall' pd' by them is	xxxiiij s' ij d'
So on Easter daye 1578 ther Remayned' in the handes' of' cleme[n]t wright and' John perry collectors	xxviij s'

There are several superfluous full points in this example which are either by way of simple decoration (as in the headings) or pen rests (as after and, *l.17). Neither they, nor the flourished dashes after the headings, are reproduced in the transcript.*

[1] ***Note the dotted*** 1 ***in the date. See also*** *l.16.* ***This is not a mixture of Roman and Arabic numerals, but a dotted form of Arabic*** 1.

[2] *There is no abbreviation sign to mark the suspension of* It[em].

FROM AN EARLY ' PARISH BOOK ', GREAT EASTON, 1578

All the officers of this parish entered their accounts and memoranda in the same book. Accounts of the ' collectors for the poore ' in summarised form are illustrated. Very few records of poor relief before the Poor Law Acts of 1597 and 1601 have survived.

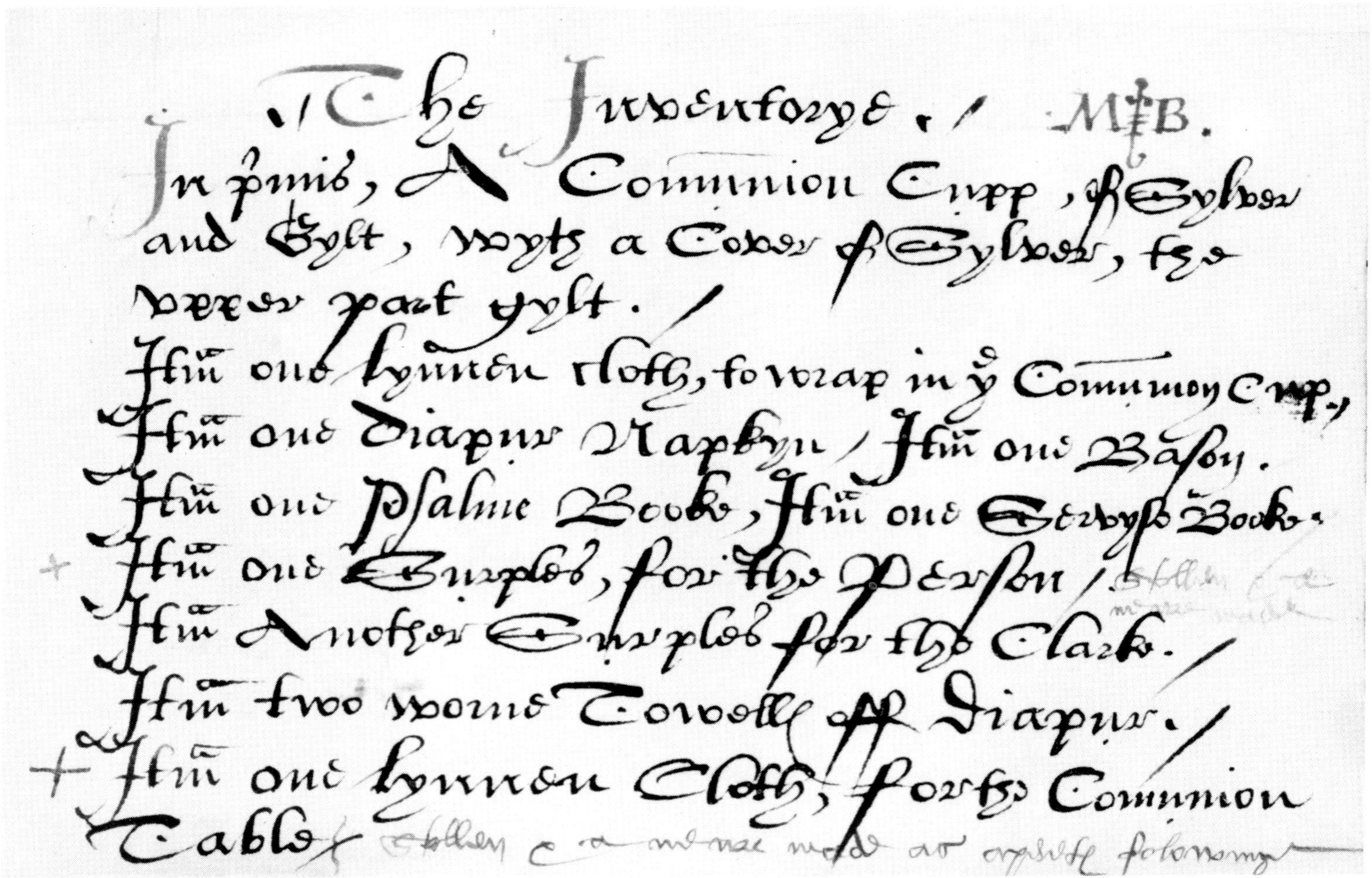

The Inventorye. / MrB.
Inprimis, A Communion Cupp, of Sylver and gylt, wyth a Cover of Sylver, the upper part gylt. /
Item one lynnen cloth, to wrap in ye Communion Cupp.
Item one diaper Napkyn / Item one Bason.
Item one Psalme Booke, Item one Servyse Booke.
Item one Surples, for the Person /
Item Another Surples for the Clark. /
Item two newe Towells off diaper. /
Item one lynnen Cloth, for the Communion Table

The Inventorye./ M/B.[1]

In p[r]*i*mis, A Com[m]union Cupp, of Sylver
and Gylt, wyth a Cover of Sylver, the
vpper part gylt. /
It[e]m[2] one lynnen cloth, to wrap in y^{e} [3] Com[m]union Cup./
It[e]m one diapur Napkyn / It[e]m one Bason.
It[e]m one Psalme Booke, It[e]m one Servyse Booke./
X It[e]m one Surples, for the Person/. Stollen & a newe made[4]
It[e]m Another Surples for the Clarke./
It[e]m two worne Towell[es][5] off diapur./
X It[e]m one lynnen Cloth, for the Comunion
Table/ Stollen & a newe made as apereth folowinge[6]

[1] *The initials of Myles Blomefyld, the churchwarden who wrote the accounts. He was an alchemist, author of* Blomfylds Quintaessens, or the Regiment of Life, *and had considerable local reputation as a " cunnyng man ". His initials, the capitals of the heading, and the first letter of l.2, are written in red.*

[2] *This is a good example of the misuse of the superscript* a *as a general mark of abbreviation. Elsewhere he abbreviated* It[em] *with the usual marks, either a flourish or a horizontal dash.*

[3] *i.e.* [th]e. *By the 16th century the rune thorn* (th), *commonly used in English documents, had become indistinguishable from* y, *and in such words as* the *and* that *(see p.10 n.1) an ordinary* y *was written.*

[4] Stollen ... made *added later.*

[5] *This writer understood the use of the looped stroke (see p.2 n.1) to represent* es. *In an entry elsewhere in the same book he wrote* seates *in full, then altered the final* es *to the looped stroke by overwriting. In another entry he wrote in close proximity two versions of the words* yeares rent*—one version in full, the other with the looped stroke replacing final* es. *It has therefore been extended* es. *He did occasionally use it as an alternative final* s *(cf. p.15 n.1).*

[6] Stollen ... folowinge *added later.*

CHURCHWARDENS' INVENTORY, CHELMSFORD, 1582

Great care was taken by some parishes to preserve church property. At Chelmsford an inventory was drawn up annually by the retiring churchwardens, entered in the account book, and checked by their successors.

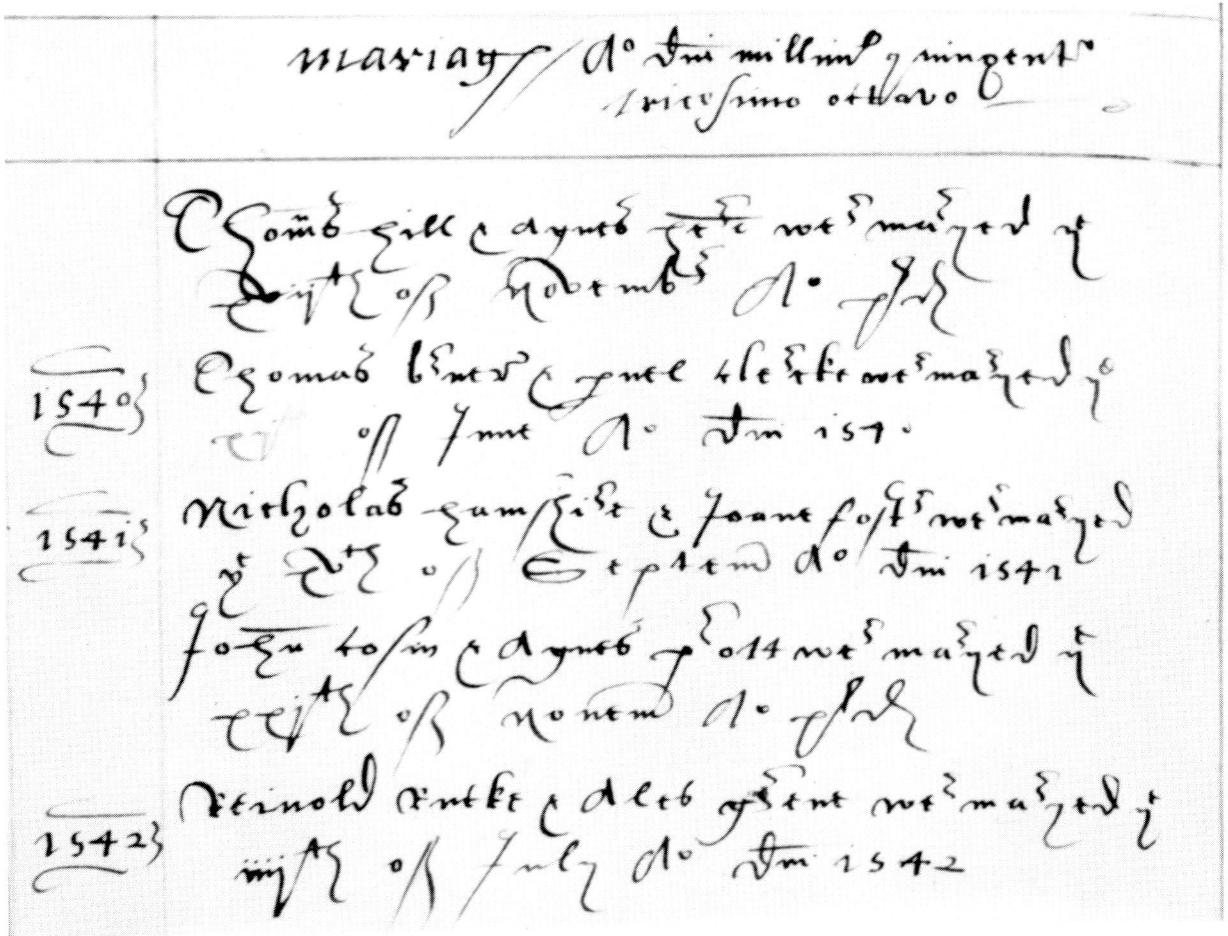

Mariages / Ao dni millimo quingentmo tricesimo octavo

Thomas Gill & Agnes [illegible] were maryed ye [illegible] of Novembr Ao predicto

1540 Thomas Bever & Jane Fletcher were maryed ye [illegible] of June Ao dni 1540

1541 Nicholas Humfrey & Joane Foster were maryed ye [illegible] of Septembr Ao dni 1541

John Tomson & Agnes [illegible] were maryed ye [illegible] of Novem Ao predicto

1542 Reinold [illegible] & Alice [illegible] were maryed ye iiijth of July Ao dni 1542

	mariag[es] / A[nn]*o* d[omi]ni mill[es]im*o* quingent[esim]*o* tricesimo octavo ————
	Thom*as*[1] hill & Agnes he^{r}d[2] we^{r} ma^{r}yed ye xvijth of' Novemb^{r} A[nn]*o* p[re]d[icto]
1540[3]	Thomas b^{r}uer & p[er]nel[4] cle^{r}cke we^{r} ma^{r}yed ye xijth of' June A[nn]*o* d[omi]ni 1540
1541	Nicholas hamshi^{r}e & Joane fost^{r} we^{r} ma^{r}yed ye xvth of' Septem[bre][5] A[nn]*o* d[omi]ni 1541
	John' cosin & Agnes p^{r}ott we^{r} ma^{r}yed ye xxjth of' Nouem[bre] A[nn]*o* p[re]d[icto]
1542	Reinold Rucke & Ales g^{r}ene we^{r} ma^{r}yed ye iiijth of' July A[nn]*o* d[omi]ni 1542

[1] *Though the* a *is superscript there is no letter omitted.*

[2] *This writer almost invariably raised his* r (*for an exception see* b^{r}uer, *l.*5) *whether there was an obvious omission* (*as* fost^{r}, *l.*7) *or not* (*as* cle^{r}cke, *l.*5); *the form* Spa^{r}row *is found elsewhere in his work. This practice is reproduced in the transcript without extension. The reading* herd *is confirmed by the writer's use on other pages of this alternative form of* d, *with the ascender sharply sloped, sometimes, as here, lying flat. The surname* Herd *is common in the parish.*

[3] *See p.*6 *n.*1. *The framing of the date is not reproduced.*

[4] *This might equally well be extended* p[ar]nel. *The writer used both forms when he gave the name in full.*

[5] *The writer consistently spelt the months as* Septembre, Octobre, Nouembre *and* Decembre *when he did not abbreviate.*

PARISH REGISTER, STANFORD RIVERS (TRANSCRIBED 1582)

Owing perhaps to the poor state of the original, a complete transcript from 1538 was made in 1582 in a paper book. In compliance with the Royal injunction another transcript, on parchment, was made in 1598, but the entries before 1558 were then omitted. A transcript on parchment for another parish is illustrated on Plate X.

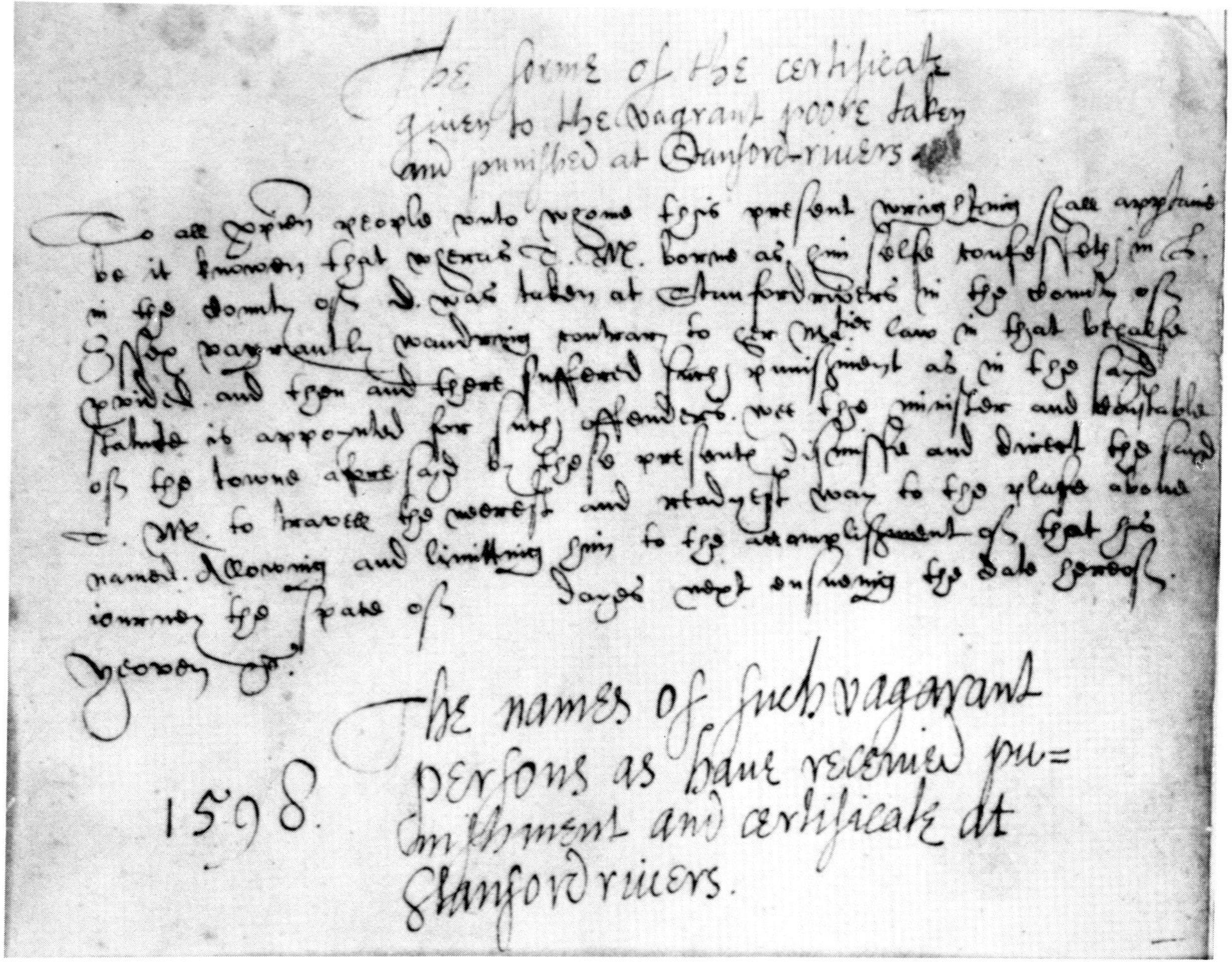

The forme of the certificat
giuen to the vagrant poore taken
and punished at Stanford-riuers

To all christian people unto whome this present writing shall appeare be it knowen that [illegible] T. M. borne as him selfe confesseth in L. in the county of D. was taken at Stanfordriuers in the county of Essex vagrantly wandering contrary to her Maties law in that behalfe provided and then and there suffered such punishment as in the said statute is appointed for such offenders. we the minister and constable of the towne aforesaid by these presents dismisse and direct the said T. M. to travell the nerest and readyest way to the place above named. Allowing and limitting him to the accomplishment of that his iourney the space of   dayes next ensuing the date hereof.
Yeoven etc.

The names of such vagarant
persons as haue receiued pu=
nishment and certificate at
Stanfordriuers.

1598

The forme of the certificate giuen to the vagrant poore taken and punished at Stanford-riuers.

To all xp'ien[1] people vnto whome this present wrighting shall app[er]taine be it knowen that wheras T. M. borne as him selfe confesseth in L. in the County of D. was taken at Stanfordrivers in the County of Essex vagrantly wandring contrary to her Maties.[2] law in that behalfe p[ro]vided and then and there suffered such punishment as in the sayd statute is appoynted for such offenders. wee the minister and Constable of the towne aforesayd by these present[es][3] dismisse and direct the sayd T.M. to travell the neerest and readyest way to the place[4] aboue named. Allowing and limitting him to the accomplishment of that his iourney the space of   dayes next ensueing the date hereof. Yeoven[5] &c'.

1598. The names of such vagarant persons as haue receiued punishment and certificate at Stanford riuers.

The downward flourish of final f *has not been reproduced in this transcript.*

[1] *i.e.* Chr[ist]ien. *Note abbreviation from Greek form, the* x *and* p *representing the letters* chi *and* rho *of the Greek alphabet.*

[2] *This should be expanded* Ma[ies]ties, *as the letter* i *still at this date commonly represented the consonantal sound now rendered by* j (*cf.* iourney, *l.*13). *The modern distinction between* i *and* j *was just beginning to be established at the end of the* 16*th century but was not generally known until much later; see the article on the letter* J *in the* Oxford English Dictionary.

[3] *It is impossible to be sure at this date whether the looped stroke signifies* es *or* s. *As the writer used final* e *and* es *fairly freely it has been extended* es. *Essex countryfolk today speak of* waspes, postes, frostes, *etc., pronouncing an extra syllable. It is a feature of Essex dialect that words ending in* -sk, -sp, -st, *commonly form their plural in* es, *see E. Gepp,* Essex Dialect Dictionary (1923), *p.*127.

[4] s *altered to* c *by overwriting.*

[5] *i.e.* given.

FORM OF VAGRANT'S CERTIFICATE, STANFORD RIVERS, 1598

As a guide for future officers this certificate was entered in the ' parish book '; it served as an authority for the vagrant's journey to the parish to which he belonged. The fact that no names were recorded on this page does not necessarily indicate an absence of vagrants.

Hayden, in Essex

A trewe Copye of all those that haue
beene Baptyzed in the paryshe of
Hayden from the yeare of or Lorde
God. 1558. yt is, from ye beggynnynge of ye
Reygne of or Soverceigne Lady Elyzabethe &c
vnto the yeare of or Lorde 1599, faythfully copyed
out accordinge to the Lawe in yt case prouyded,
and so contynued orderly for the yeares folowinge

By Thomas Newcome

1558

1558 Elizabeth Browne was baptized the nynteenth day of Januarye — J Browne

Anno Dni 1559

Elizabeth Syme was baptized the — Syme

1

Hayden, in Essex

A trewe Copye of all those that haue
beene Baptyzed in the paryshe of
Hayden from the yeare of o[u]*r* Lorde
God. 1558. y^{t}[1] is, from ye begynnynge of y^{e}
Reygne of o[u]*r* Sovereigne Lady Elyzabethe. &c'
vnto the yeare of o[u]*r* Lorde 1599, faythfully copyed
out accordinge to the Lawe in y^{t} case prouyded,
and so contynued orderly for the yeares folowinge

By Thomas Newcome[n][2]

1558

1558 Elizabeth Browne was baptized the— nynetenth day of of[3] January ——— } Browne

Anno D[omi]ni 1559

1559 Elizabeth Kynge was baptized the eyght day of June ——————— } Kynge

[1] *i.e.* [th][a]t; *the* y *represents* th (*see p.7 n.3*) *and the omission of* a *is shown by the superscript* t.
[2] *Rector*, 1588-1625.
[3] of *repeated.*

PARCHMENT TRANSCRIPT OF HEYDON REGISTER, 1599

Taking advantage of the wording of the injunction of 1598 requiring registers to be copied on parchment from the beginning, ' but more especially since the first year of her Majesty's reign ', the rector has only copied from 1558. The paper register from 1538, from which this was copied, is one of the few originals which have also survived.

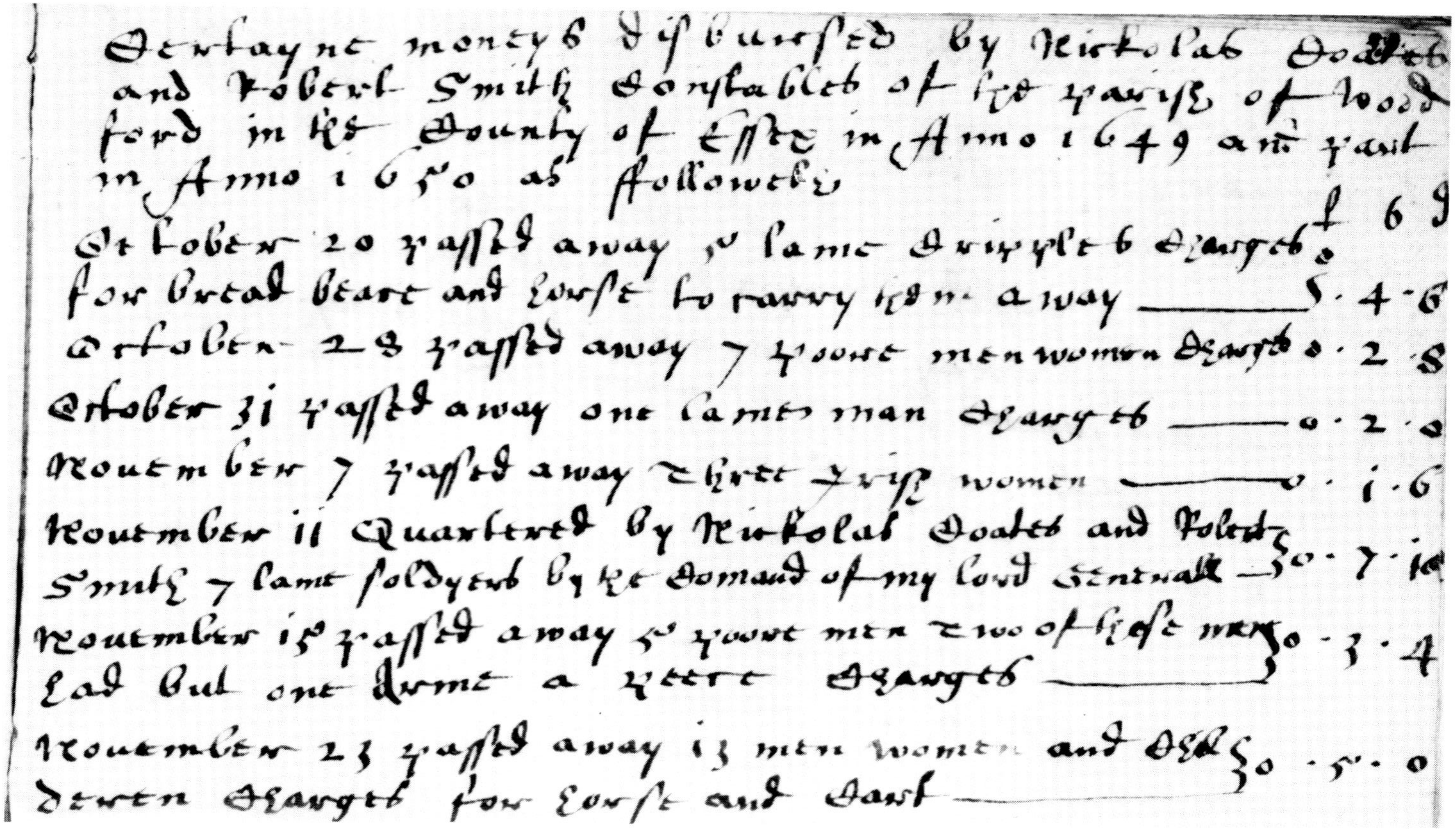
Certayne moneys disbursed by Nicholas Coales and Robert Smith Constables of the parish of Wood ford in the County of Essex in Anno 1649 and part in Anno 1650 as followeth

£ s d

October 20 passed away ye lame cripple charges 0
for bread beare and horse to carry him away — 5 · 4 · 6
October 28 passed away 7 poore men women charges 0 · 2 · 8
October 31 passed away one lame man charges — 0 · 2 · 0
November 7 passed away three Irish women — 0 · 1 · 6
November 11 Quartered by Nicholas Coales and Robert
Smith 7 lame soldyers by the Comand of my lord Generall — 0 · 7 · 10
November 15 passed away 5 poore men two of these men
had but one arme a peece charges — 0 · 3 · 4
November 23 passed away 13 men women and chil
dren charges for horse and cart — 0 · 5 · 0

Certayne moneys disbursed by Nickolas Coates and Robert Smith Constables of the parish of Wood ford in the County of Essex in Anno 1649 and part in Anno 1650 as Followeth

	l'	s	d
October 20 passed away 5 lame Cripples Charges for bread beare and horse to carry them away ————	0	4	6
October 28 passed away 7 poore men women Charges	0	2	8
October 31[1] passed away one lame man Charges ————	0	2	0
Nouember 7 passed away Three Irish women ————	0	1	6
Nouember 11 Quartered by Nickolas Coates and Robert Smith 7 lame soldyers by the Comand of my lord Generall —	0	7	10
Nouember 15 passed away 5 poore men Two of those men had but one Arme a peece Charges ————	0	3	4
Nouember 23 passed away 13 men women and Chil deren Charges for horse and Cart ————	0	5	0

[1] *See p.6 n.1.*

CONSTABLES' ACCOUNTS, WOODFORD, 1649

Poor travellers passing through the parish on authorised journeys were usually relieved by the constables. By the end of the eighteenth century the frequency of payments and the number of forged 'passes' in circulation often led the overseers to curb such expenditure.

196

At ye said Vestrie held Septemr: ye 3rd 1658.

It is also agreed, that Foster Dickinson ye present
Sexton shall have [redacted] seaventeen shillings and
six pence every quarter of a yeare during his con=
tinuance in the place for the well looking to the
Clock, the Chimes, and finding oyle for them, and
ringing the eight and foure a clock bell from x
Michaelmas to our Lady-day every yeare, accor=
ding to the former custome, and also for the cleane
keeping and setting of the Church, and perform=
ing all other duties belonging to the office of the
Sexton, and not to lend any Utensills belonging
to the Church without the consent of the Church=
wardens, the above named allowance to begin
at or from our Lady-day last past.

At y^e said Vestrie held Septem^r: y^e 2. 1658. 196

It is also agreed, that Joseph Dickinson y^e present Sextan shall have [1] seaventeen shillings and six pence every quarter of a yeere (during his continuance in the place) for the well lookeing to the Clock, the Chimes, and findeing oyle for them, and ringing the eighth and foure a clock-bell from × Michaelmas to our Lady-day every yeer, according to the former custome, and also for the cleane keeping and sweeping of the Church, and performeing all other duties belonging to the office of the Sextan, and not to lend any Utensills belonging to the Church without the consent of the Churchwardens, the above named allowance to begin at or from our Lady-day last past.

[1] *Deletion*

THE SEXTON'S DUTIES, WALTHAM HOLY CROSS, 1658

This resolution is entered in the churchwardens' account book as a precedent. The contemporary vestry book, no longer extant, was probably reserved for such resolutions as needed the confirmation of the justices, who were not concerned with church officers.

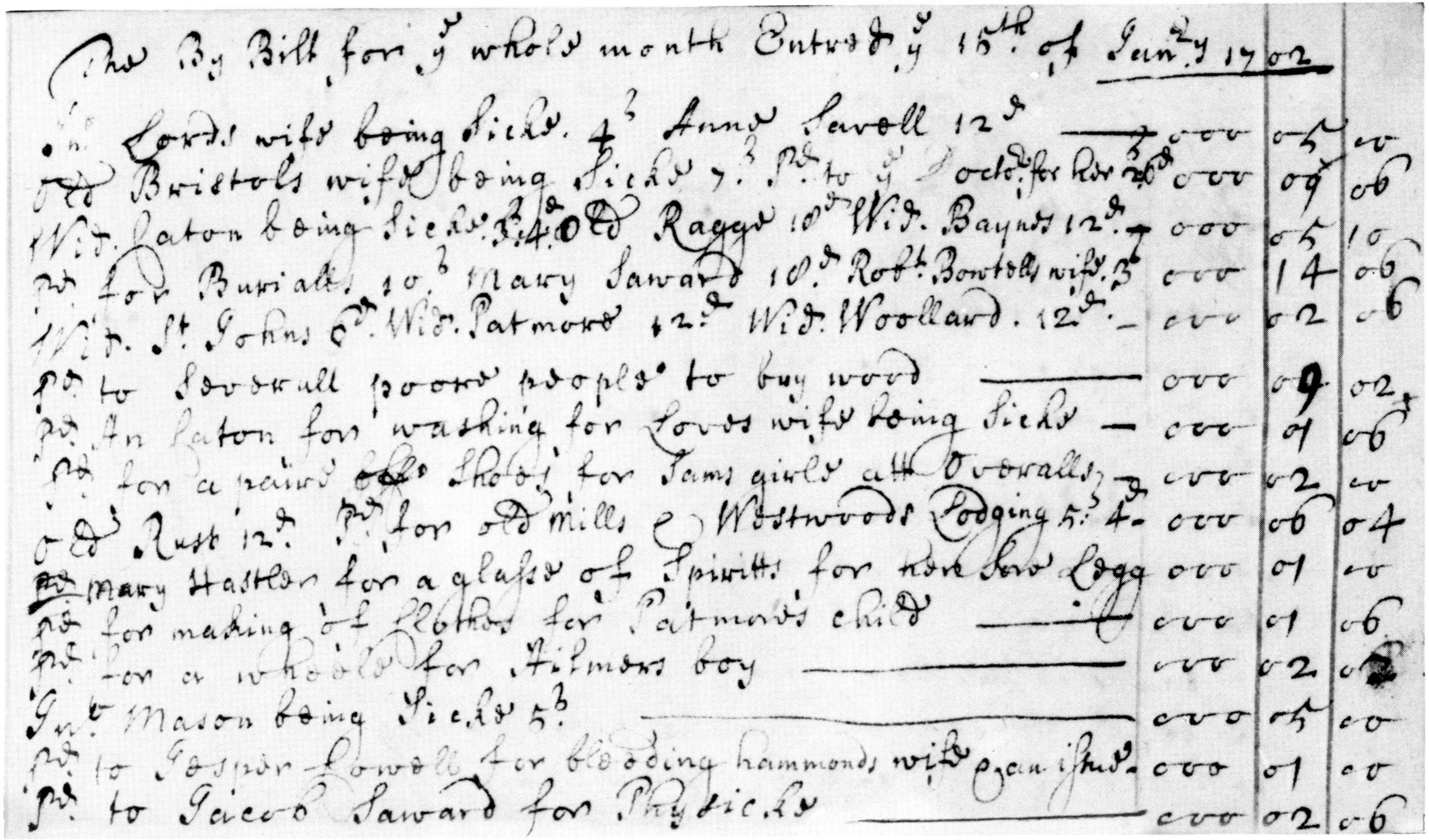

The By Bill for ye whole month Entred ye 15th of Jan.ry 1702			
In Lords wife being Sicke 4s Anne Savell 12d	000	05	00
Old Bristols wife being Sicke 7s Pd to ye Doctr for her 2s 6d	000	09	06
Wid. Eaton being Sicke 3s 4d Old Ragge 10d Wid. Baynes 12d	000	05	10
Pd for Buriall 10s Mary Saward 10d Robt. Bowtells wife 3s 8d	000	14	06
Wid. St. Johns 6d Wid. Patmore 12d Wid. Woollard 12d	000	02	06
Pd to Severall poore people to buy wood	000	09	02
Pd An Eaton for washing for Lords wife being Sicke	000	01	06
Pd for a paire of Shoes for Sams girle att Overalls	000	02	00
Old Rust 12d Pd for old Mills & Westwoods Lodging 5s 4d	000	06	04
Pd Mary Hastler for a glasse of Spiritts for her Sore Legg	000	01	00
Pd for making of Clothes for Patmores child	000	01	06
Pd for a whole for Ailmors boy	000	02	06
Goodw Mason being Sicke 5s	000	05	00
Pd to Gaspar Lowell for blooding hammonds wife eqa. ished	000	01	00
Pd to Jacob Saward for Physicke	000	02	06

The By Bill for y^{e} **whole** month **Entred** ye 15th. of Jan^{ry}. 17		02[1]	
Jno. Lords wife being Sicke. 4^{s} Anne Savell 12^{d} ————	000	05	00
Old Bristols wife being Sicke 7^{s}. P^{d}. to ye Docto^{r}. for her 2^{s}:6^{d}	000	09^{x}	06
Wid. Caton being Sicke. 3^{s}:4^{d}: Old Ragge 18^{d} Wid. Baynes 12^{d}. —	000	05	10
P^{d}. for Burialls 10^{s}. Mary Saward 18^{d}. Robt. Bowtells wife. 3^{s}	000	14	06
Wid. S^{t}. Johns 6^{d}. Wid. Patmore 12^{d}. Wid. Woollard. 12^{d}. ————	000	02	06
P^{d}. to Severall poore people to buy wood ————	000	09	02
P^{d}. An Caton for washing for Loves wife being Sicke ————	000	01	06^{x}
P^{d}. for a paire off Shoes for Sams girle att Overalls ————	000	02	00
Old Rust 12^{d}. P^{d}. for old Mills & Westwoods Lodging 5^{s}:4^{d} ————	000	06	04
P^{d}. Mary Hastler for a glasse of Spiritts for her Sore Legg	000	01	00
P^{d} for making of Clothes for Patmores child ————	000	01	06
P^{d}. for a wheele for Ailmers boy ————	000	02	02[2]
Jno. Mason being Sicke 5^{s}. ————	000	05	00
P^{d}. to Jesper Cowell for bleeding hammonds wife & an issue ————	000	01	00
P^{d} to Jacob Saward for Physicke ————	000	02	06

[1] *From the late* 12*th century Lady Day,* 25 *March, was generally accepted in England as the opening of the year, and continued so, officially, till* 1752, *when* 1 *January was adopted instead. This bill, therefore, which is dated* 15 *January* 1702, *would be dated* 1703 *according to modern reckoning.*

[2] 6 *deleted and* 2 *overwritten.*

RELIEF OF THE POOR, THAXTED, 1703

Relief was by no means limited to cash payments but could take such forms as grants in kind, medical attention, or exemption from payment of rates. The ' By bill ' represented relief given to the casual poor in contrast to regular weekly relief paid to ' pensioners ', such as the aged and incurable sick.

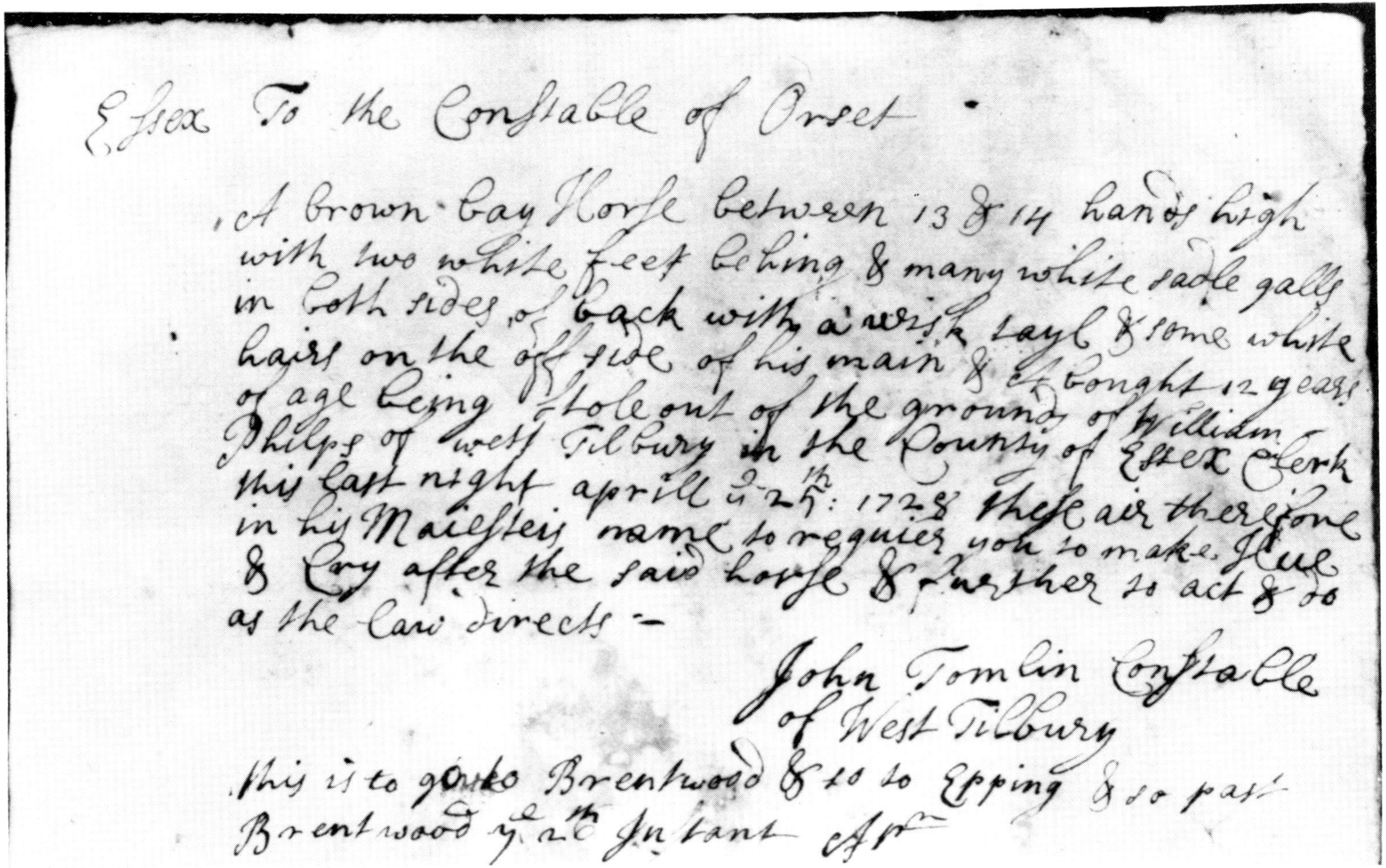

Essex To the Constable of Orset

A brown bay Horse between 13 & 14 hands high
with two white feet behing & many white sadle galls
in both sides of back with a wisk tayl & some white
hairs on the off side of his main & thought 12 years
of age being stole out of the grounds of William
Philps of west Tilbury in the County of Essex Clerk
this last night aprill ye 25th: 1728 these air ther sfore
in his Maiesteis name to requier you to make Hue
& Cry after the said horse & further to act & do
as the law directs —

John Tomlin Constable
of West Tilbury

this is to go to Brentwood & to to Epping & so past
Brentwood ye 26th Instant Apr

Essex

To the Constable of Orset

A brown bay Horse between 13 & 14 hands high with two white feet behing & many white sadle galls in both sides of back with a wisk tayl & some white hairs on the off side of his main & Abought 12 years of age being stole out of the grounds of William Philps of west Tilbury in the County of Essex Clerk this last night aprill ye 25th: 1728 these air therefore in his Maiesteis name to requier you to make Hue & Cry after the said horse & further to act & do as the law directs —

John Tomlin Constable
of West Tilbury

this is to go to[1] Brentwood & so to Epping & so past Brentwood ye 26th Instant Ap^{r}

[1] Give *deleted* ; go to *overwritten*.

A 'HUE AND CRY', WEST TILBURY, 1728

The pursuit of robbers by a 'hue and cry' in the King's name dates from the Statute of Winchester of 1285. The fact that the loser could obtain redress by a fine levied against the Hundred in which the robbery took place ensured that it was taken seriously. Here, the constable of West Tilbury passes the information to his neighbour at Orsett and suggests the route that the pursuit should follow. The document apparently failed to complete its journey, for it was found at Theydon Garnon.

An acco.^t of the Several Disburstm^ts made by Us Robt Swan James Wells & Wm Sparks Survey^rs of the Highways of Ashdon from Christmas 1734 to the 12th of December 1735 as followeth

		£	s	d
By Robt Swan				
1734 March 20	p^d Tho. Symonds for picking two Load & a half of Stones	0.	2.	6
21	p^d for my return at the Sessions	0.	0.	6
1735 June	p^d John Marsh & Jno Warren for diging of Gravell six days apeice at 2.^s 2^d p^r day	0.	13.	0
Octo^r	p^d Henry Sale for putting down the Stiles in Stephen Adams fields that were taken Up to carry Gravel into the Road	0.	0.	4

An acco^{t}. of the Several Disburstm^{ts} made by vs Robt. Swan James[1] Wells & Wm Sparks Survey^{r}s of the Highways of Ashdon from Christmas 1734 to the 12th. of December 1735 as followeth

P[er] Robt: Swan

	£	s	d
1734			
March 20 p^{d} Tho. Symonts for picking two Load & a half of stones ——	0.	2.	6
21 p^{d} for my return at the Sessions ————	0.	0.	6
1735			
June—p^{d} John Marsh & Jno Warren for diging of Gravell six days a peice at 2^{s}. 2^{d} p[er] day ————	0.	13.	0
Octo^{r}—p^{d} Henry Sale for putting down the Stiles in Stephen Adams fields that were taken vp to carry Gravel into the Road——	0.	0.	4

[1] *Note use of looped stroke as final* s; *see also* stones, *l.5*, Stiles, *l.9, and p.2 n.1*.

REPAIRING THE ASHDON HIGHWAYS, 1734-5

Theoretically no cash need have been handled by the surveyors of the highways as they could call on the inhabitants to provide labour and carts. In practice many compounded for these obligations; a rate was only levied if the 'statute duty' was found insufficient to carry out necessary repairs. Before the advent of macadamized surfaces accounts were mainly long lists of stones and gravel supplied to fill up the ruts.

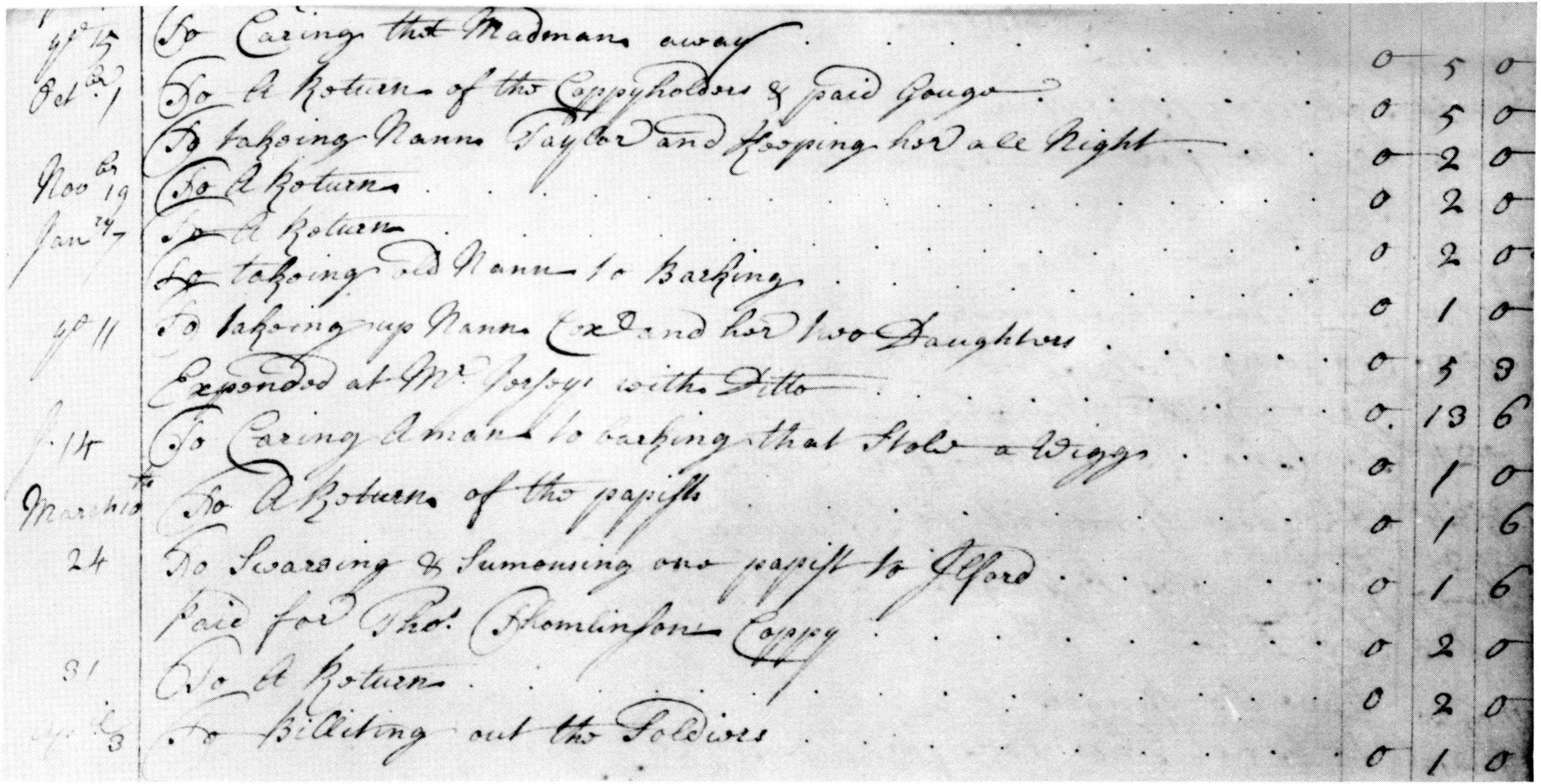

17[??]15	To Caring that Madman away	0	5	0
Oct.ber 1	To a Roturn of the Coppyholders & paid Gouge	0	5	0
	To takeing Nann Taylor and Keeping her ale Night	0	2	0
Nov.ber 19	To a Roturn	0	2	0
Jan.ry 7	To a Roturn	0	2	0
	To takeing old Nann to Barking	0	1	0
[??] 11	To takeing up Nann Cox and her two Daughters	0	5	3
	Expended at Mr. Joseys with Ditto	0	13	6
[??] 14	To Caring a man to barking that Stole a Wigg	0	1	0
March 10	To a Roturn of the papists	0	1	6
24	To Swareing & Sumoning one papist to Ilford	0	1	6
	Paid for Tho.s Thomlinson Coppy	0	2	0
31	To a Roturn	0	2	0
[??] 3	To Billiting out the Soldiers	0	1	0

yᵉ 15	To Caring thet Madman away	0	5	0
Octᵇʳ. 1	To A Return of the Coppyholders & paid Gouge	0	5	0
	To takeing Nann Taylor and keeping her all Night	0	2	0
Novᵇʳ 19	To A Return	0	2	0
Janʳʸ 7	To A Return	0	2	0
	To takeing old Nann to Barking	0	1	0
yᵉ 11	To takeing up Nann Cox and her two Daughters	0	5	3
	Expended at Mʳ. Jerseys with Ditto	0	13	6
J. 14	To Caring A man to barking that stole a Wigg	0	1	0
March 10ᵗʰ	To A Return of the papists	0	1	6
24	To Swareing & Sumensing one papist to Ilford	0	1	6
	Paid for Thoˢ. Thomlinson Coppy	0	2	0
31	To A Return	0	2	0
Apⁱˡ. 3	To Billiting out the Soldiers	0	1	0

CONSTABLES' ACCOUNTS, EAST HAM, 1743

The multifarious duties of the constable made his task probably the most unpopular of all parish offices. His accounts often reflect national history; these illustrate the restrictive measures taken against the papists as a result of Jacobite intrigues.

TRANSLATIONS

Grant of Land, Little Waltham, *c.*1275

Let present and future know that I William de la Grave of Little Waltham have granted given and by this my present charter confirmed to William Russel merchant of Chelmsford for his homage and service and for twenty and four shillings of sterlings [silver pennies] which he gave me as a fine two acres of my land with all their appurtenances in Little Waltham lying in a certain croft which is called Langecroft as it is enclosed by hedges and ditches between the land of John of Belsted [in Broomfield] which is called la Reden [?Long Ridden, Great Waltham] on the one part and the lane leading from the King's highway to the grove of Geoffrey of Belsted on the other whereof one head abuts on the curtilage of the said John and the other head on my messuage, to have and to hold to the said William and his heirs or his assigns or their heirs of me and my heirs or my assigns, and whenever and to whomsoever he shall wish to give sell bequeath mortgage or any other way assign the said two acres of land with their appurtenances except to religious men and Jews, freely quietly well and in peace by right and by way of inheritance for ever, paying in respect thereof annually to me and my heirs or my assigns, he and his heirs or his assigns, 8d. at two terms of the year namely at Easter 4d. and at the feast of St. Michael 4d. for all secular services customs suits of courts and all secular demands saving the service of the lord King when it shall fall due more or less one farthing. And I the said William and my heirs or my assigns will warrant defend and acquit the said two acres of land with their appurtenances to the said William and his heirs or his assigns or their heirs as is aforesaid by the aforenamed service against all men and women for ever. And that this my grant gift and confirmation firm and stable may remain for ever I have set my seal to this present charter. These being witnesses, Robert de Haylesden, Roger of Wimbish, Geoffrey of Belsted, Richard Koc, Sewell of Springfield, Richard de Munchanesy, Stephen le Franceis and others.

*See p.*1.

Title Deed of Charitable Income, Harlow, 1324

Let present and future know that I William of Mashbury in the county of Essex have given granted and by this my present charter confirmed to Master John of Stanton clerk, three shillings of annual rent to be received annually at two terms of the year by equal portions at the feast of St. Michael and at Easter from John son of Stephen of Paris for twelve acres of arable land and two acres of meadow which he held of me in the village of Great Parndon lying in a field called Wedhey in the said village between Parndon Wood on the one part and the land of Walter Cook [' Cocus '] on the other, and one head abuts on Farnhel and the other head on the common way which leads from Ryhel [Rye Hill] towards Waltham, to have and to hold the aforesaid three shillings with homages, wardships, escheats, reliefs, marriages and all other things pertaining to the said rent to the said Master John of Stanton his heirs and assigns of the chief lord of that fee by the services by right from it due and accustomed. And I the aforesaid William of Mashbury my heirs and assigns the aforesaid three shillings of annual rent with homages, wardships, escheats, reliefs, marriages, and all other things to the said rent pertaining to the said Master John of Stanton his heirs and assigns against all men will warrant for ever. In witness whereof I have set my seal to this present charter. These being witnesses, Thomas de Cann [*or* Caun; *an associated deed gives* Cavnne], Gilbert ate Chambre, Geoffrey Maulle, James of Weald, John of Weald, John Campyon and others. Given at Harlow the ninth day of April in the seventeenth year of the reign of King Edward son of King Edward.

*See p.*2.

PART II

EXAMPLES FROM OTHER ESSEX ARCHIVES

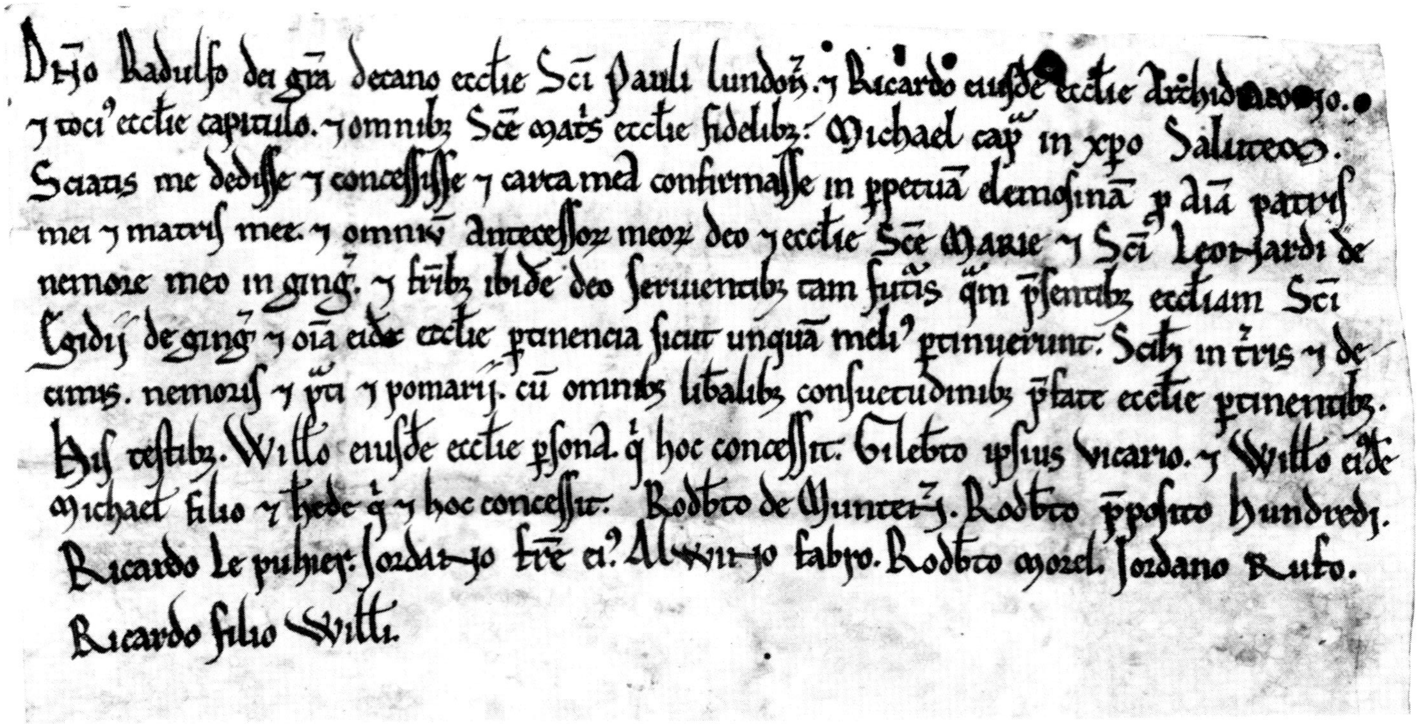
Dn̄o Radulfo dei gr̄a decano ecclie Sci Pauli Lundon. 7 Ricardo eiusdē ecclie archidiacono.
7 toci ecclie capitulo. 7 omnibꝫ Scē matris ecclie fidelibꝫ: Michael cap in xpo Salutem.
Sciatis me dedisse 7 concessisse 7 carta mea confirmasse in ppetuā elemosinā p aīa patris
mei 7 matris mee. 7 omniū antecessoꝝ meoꝝ deo 7 ecclie Scē Marie 7 Sci Leonardi de
nemore meo in ging. 7 frībꝫ ibidē deo seruientibꝫ tam futuris qm p̄sentibꝫ ecclesiam Sci
Egidii de ging 7 oīa eidē ecclie ptinencia sicut unquā melius ptinuerunt. Scilꝫ in tris 7 de
cimis. nemoribus 7 pti 7 pomariis. cū omnibꝫ libalibꝫ consuetudinibꝫ p̄fate ecclie ptinentibꝫ.
His testibꝫ. Willo eiusdē ecclie psona. qi hoc concessit. Gileberto ipsius vicario. 7 Willo eidē
Michael filio 7 herede qi 7 hoc concessit. Rodbto de Munteri. Rodbto pposito hundredi.
Ricardo le puhier. Iordano frē ei9. Alwino fabro. Rodbto morel. Iordano Rufo.
Ricardo filio Willi.

D[omi]No Radulfo dei gr[ati]a decano eccl[es]ie S[an]c[t]i Pauli lundon'. [et] Ricardo eiusde[m] eccl[es]ie archidiacoNo. [et] toci[us] eccl[es]ie capitulo. [et] omnib[us] S[an]c[t]e Mat[r]*is* eccl[es]ie fidelib[us]; Michael cap[r]*a* in Chr[ist]o[1] SaluteM. Sciatis me dedisse [et] concessisse [et] carta mea confirmasse in p[er]petua[m] elemosina[m] p[ro] a[n]i[m]a patris mei [et] matris mee. [et] omniv[m] antecessor[um] meor[um] deo [et] eccl[es]ie S[an]c[t]e MARie [et] S[an]c[t]i LeoNardi de nemore meo in ging'. [et] fr[atr]ib[us] ibide[m] deo seruientib[us] tam fut[ur]is[2] q[u]*a*m p[re]sentib[us] eccl[es]iam S[an]c[t]i Egidij de ging' [et] o[mn]ia eide[m] eccl[es]ie p[er]tinencia sicut unqua[m] meli[us] p[er]tinuerunt. Scil[ic][et] in t[er]ris [et] decimis. nemoris [et] p[r]*a*ti [et] pomarij. cu[m] omnib[us] lib[er]alib[us] consuetudinib[us] p[re]fate eccl[es]ie p[er]tinentib[us]. His testib[us]. Will[elm]o eiusde[m] eccl[es]ie p[er]sona. q[u]*i* hoc concessit. Gileb[er]to ipsius vicario. [et] Will[elm]o ei[us]de[m] Michael[is] filio [et] h[er]ede q[u]*i* [et] hoc concessit. Rodb[er]to de MunteN'. Rodb[er]to p[re]posito Hundredj. Ricardo Le puhier. JordaNo fr[atr]e ei[us]. AlwiNo fabro. Rodb[er]to Morel. Jordano Rufo. Ricardo filio Will[elm]i.

Translation below.

Slightly reduced.

[1] *Note abbreviation of* Chr[ist]o *from Greek form,* x *and* p *representing the letters* chi *and* rho *of the Greek alphabet. For its use in English, see p.*9 *n.*1.

[2] *Note form of special sign denoting omission of* ur. *Cf. p.*1 *n.*3.

To Lord Ralph, by the grace of God dean of the church of St. Paul, London, and to Richard, archdeacon of the same church, and to the chapter of the whole church, and to all the faithful of Holy Mother Church, Michael Capra [sends] greeting in Christ. Know that I have given and granted and confirmed by my charter, in perpetual alms for the soul of my father and my mother and of all my ancestors, to God and the church of St. Mary and St. Leonard in my wood of Ginges [Mountnessing], and to the brothers there serving God, both future and present, the church of St. Giles in Ginges and all the appurtenances to that church, such as ever at best belonged to it; that is to say in lands and tithes of wood and meadow and orchard, with all free customs belonging to the aforesaid church. These being witnesses, William parson of the same church, who has agreed to this, Gilbert his vicar, and William son and heir of the same Michael, who also granted this, Robert de Mounteney, Robert bailiff of the hundred, Richard le Puhier, Jordan his brother, Alwin the smith, Robert Morel, Jordan Rufus, Richard son of William.

NOTIFICATION OF GIFT, MOUNTNESSING, *circa* 1152

Michael Capra, founder of Thoby Priory in Mountnessing, adds to its endowments the church of St. Giles, Mountnessing, which remained appropriated to the Priory till the Dissolution.

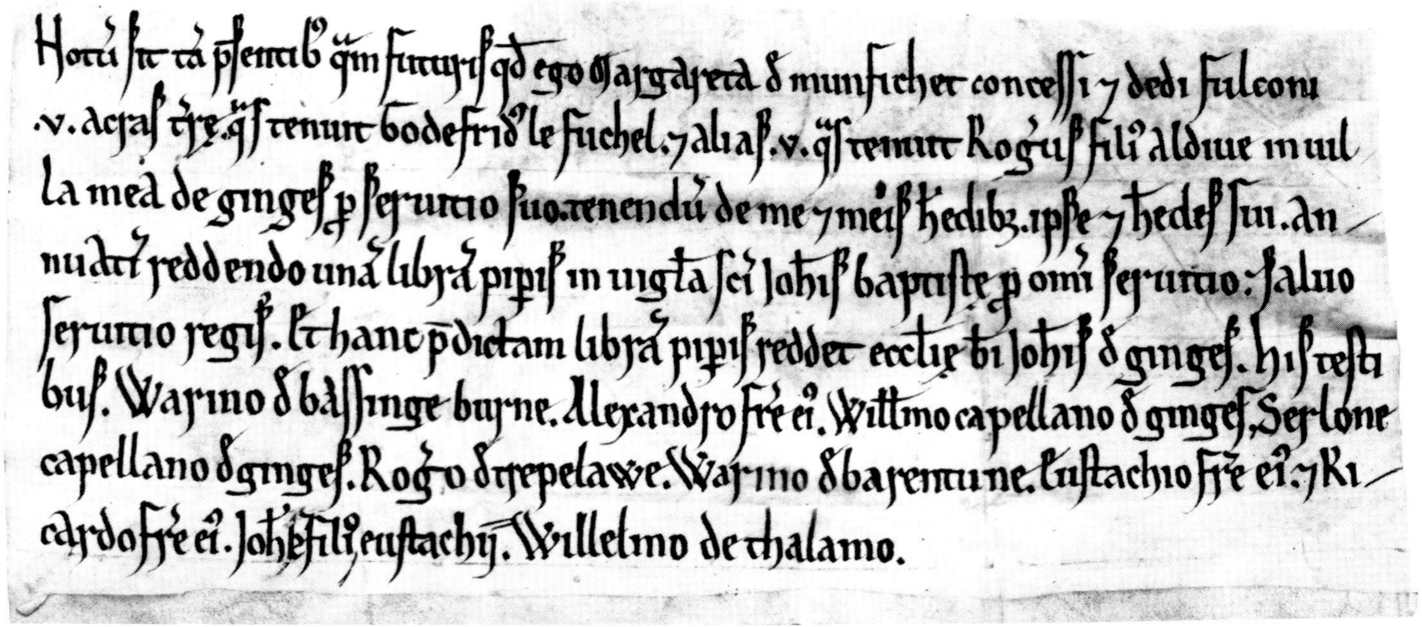
Notum sit tam presentibus quam futuris quod ego Margareta de Munfichet concessi et dedi Fulconi
v. acras terre quas tenuit Godefridus le Fuchel, et alias v. quas tenuit Rogerus filius Aldiue in uil
la mea de Ginges pro seruitio suo. tenendum de me et meis heredibus. ipse et heredes sui. an
nuatim reddendo unam libram piperis in uigilia sancti Iohannis baptiste pro omni seruitio: saluo
seruitio regis. Et hanc predictam libram piperis reddet ecclesie beati Iohannis de Ginges. His testi
bus. Warino de Bassingeburne. Alexandro fratre eius. Willelmo capellano de Ginges. Serlone
capellano de Ginges. Rogero de Trepelawe. Warino de Barentune. Eustachio fratre eius. et Ri
cardo fratre eius. Iohanne filio Eustachii. Willelmo de Thalamo.

Notu[m][1] sit ta[m] p[re]sentib[us] q[u]*a*m futuris q[uo]d ego Margareta d[e] munfichet concessi [et] dedi fulconi .v. acras t[er]re[2] q[u]*a*s tenuit Godefrid[us] le fuchel. [et] alias .v. q[u]*a*s tenuit Rog[er]us fili[us] aldiue in uilla mea de ginges p[ro] seruitio suo. tenendu[m] de me [et] meis h[er]edib[us]. ipse [et] h[er]edes sui. annuati[m] reddendo una[m] libra[m] pip[er]is in uig[i]l[i]a s[an]c[t]i Joh[ann]is baptiste p[ro] om[n]i seruitio; saluo seruitio regis. Et hanc p[re]dictam libra[m] pip[er]is reddet eccl[es]ie b[eat]i Joh[ann]is d[e] ginges. His testibus. Warino d[e] bassingeburne. Alexandro fr[atr]e ei[us]. Will[el]mo capellano d[e] ginges. Serlone capellano d[e] ginges. Rog[er]o d[e] trepelawe. Warino d[e] barentune. Eustachio fr[atr]e ei[us]. [et] Ricardo fr[atr]e ei[us]. Joh[ann]e[3] filio[4] eustachij. Willelmo de thalamo.

Translation below.

Slightly reduced.

[1] ***Note form** of this general mark of abbreviation, commonly found in the 12th and early **13th centuries, and an alternative** to that described on p.1 n.4. Its use in* t[er]re *and* Rog[er]us, *1.2, **anticipates** its subsequent development, as handwriting became more current, into the special sign denoting omission of* er *described on p.1 n.6.*

[2] *Note tailed* e, *found mostly in the 12th century, **replacing the** diphthong* æ. ***After** about* 1200 *the Latin* æ *is commonly **represented** in medieval documents **by*** e.

[3] Joh[anne]s *altered to* Joh[ann]e *by scratching out* s.

[4] fili[us] *altered to* fili[o] *by changing special sign for* us (*cf.* ei[us] ***in the same line***) *to* o *and adding an omission mark.*

Be it known [to all men] both present and to come that I, Margaret de Munfichet, have granted and given to Fulk 5 acres of land which Godfrey le Fuchel held and 5 other [acres] which Roger son of Aldiva held in my vill of Ginges in return for his service, he and his heirs to hold of me and my heirs by paying annually one pound of pepper on the vigil of St. John the Baptist for all service saving the King's service. And this aforesaid pound of pepper he shall pay to the church of St. John in Ginges. These being witnesses, Warren of Bassingbourne, Alexander his brother, William chaplain of Ginges, Serlo chaplain of Ginges, Roger of Thriplow, Warren of Barrington, Eustace his brother and Richard his brother, John son of Eustace, William of the Chamber.

GRANT OF LAND, FRYERNING, *circa* 1170

Pepper was an extremely expensive commodity in the middle ages, usually brought to England by Genoese merchants with other luxuries, such as silk and cloths of gold. Rents in pepper are often found in medieval agreements. The feast of the Nativity of St. John the Baptist (which is still one of the English quarter-days) falls on 24 June, and the vigil the day before.

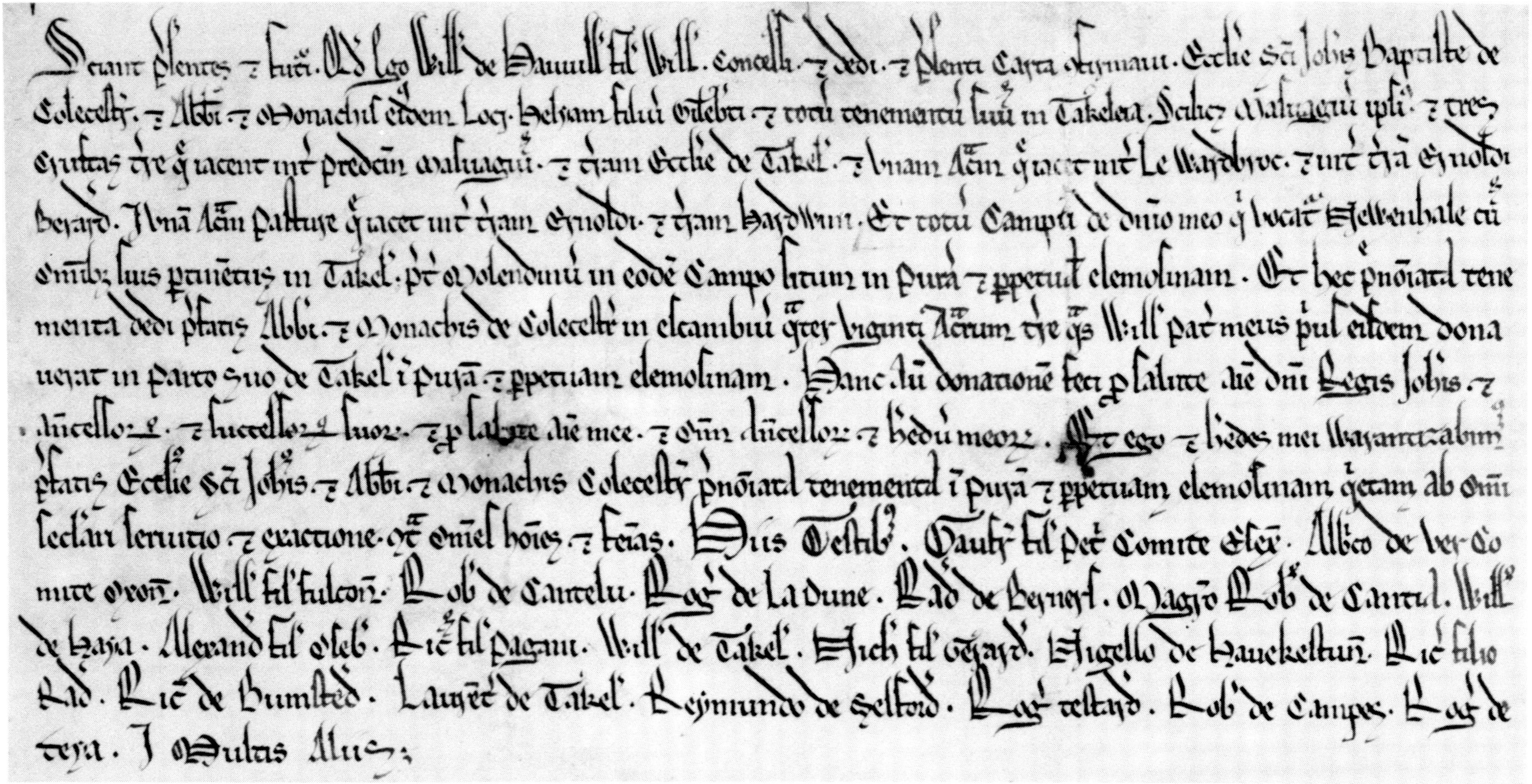

Sciant presentes et futuri. quod Ego Willelmus de Haiuill' filius Willelmi. concessi et dedi. et presenti Carta confirmaui. Ecclesie Sancti Johannis Baptiste de Colecestr'. et Abbati et Monachis eiusdem Loci. Helsam filium Gileberti et totum tenementum suum in Takeleia. Scilicet Masuagium ipsius. et tres Cunitas terre que iacent inter predictum masuagium. et terram Ecclesie de Takel'. et unam Acram que iacet inter Le Wardbroc. et inter terram Ernoldi Beiard. Et unam Acram pasture que iacet inter terram Ernoldi. et terram Hardwini. Et totum Campum de dominio meo qui uocatur Helvenhale cum omnibus suis pertinentiis in Takel'. preter Molendinum in eodem Campo situm in puram et perpetuam elemosinam. Et hec prenominata tenementa dedi prefatis Abbati et Monachis de Colecestr' in escambium quarterii viginti Acrarum terre quas Willelmus pater meus prius eisdem donauerat in parco suo de Takel' in puram et perpetuam elemosinam. Hanc autem donationem feci pro salute anime domini Regis Johannis. et antecessorum et successorum suorum. et pro salute anime mee. et omnium antecessorum et heredum meorum. Et ego et heredes mei warantizabimus prefatis Ecclesie Sancti Johannis. et Abbati et Monachis Colecestr' prenominata tenementa in puram et perpetuam elemosinam quietam ab omni seculari seruitio et exactione. contra omnes homines et feminas. Hiis Testibus. Galfrido filio Petri Comite Essex. Alberico de Ver Comite Oxon'. Willelmo filio Fulconis. Roberto de Cantelu. Rogero de La Dune. Radulfo de Berners. Magistro Roberto de Cantel'. Willelmo de Haia. Alexandro filio Oseberti. Ricardo filio Pagani. Willelmo de Takel'. Michaele filio Gerardi. Nigello de Hanckeltun'. Ricardo filio Rad'. Ricardo de Bumsted. Laurentio de Takel'. Reymundo de Selford. Rogero Teltard. Roberto de Campes. Rogero de Tey. et Multis Aliis.

Sciant p[re]sentes [et] fut[ur]i.Q[uo]d Ego Will[elmus] de Hauuill' fil[ius] Will[elmi].Concessi.[et] dedi.[et] p[re]senti Carta [con]firmaui.Eccl[es]ie S[an]c[t]i Joh[ann]is Baptiste de
Colecestr'.[et] Abb[at]i.[et] Monachis ei[us]dem Locj.Helyam[1] filiu[m] Gileb[er]ti.[et] totu[m] tenementu[m] suu[m] in Takeleia.Scilic[et] Masuagiu[m] ipsi[us].[et] tres
Cruftas t[er]re q[u]*e*[2] iacent int[er] pred[i]c[tu]m Masuagiu[m].[et] t[er]ram Eccl[es]ie de Takel[eia].[et] vnam Ac[r]*am* q[u]*e* iacet int[er] Le Wardbroc.[et] int[er] t[er]ra[m] Ernoldi
Berard'.[Et] vna[m] Ac[r]*am* pasture q[u]*e* iacet int[er] t[er]ram Ernoldi.[et] t[er]ram Hardwini.Et totu[m] Campu[m] de d[omi]nio meo q[u]*i* vocat[ur] Newenhale cu[m]
Om[n]ib[us] suis p[er]tine[n]tiis in Takel[eia].p[re]t[er] Molendinu[m] in eode[m] Campo situm in pura[m] [et] p[er]petua[m] elemosinam.Et hec p[r]*e*no[m]i[n]ata tene
menta dedi p[re]fatis Abb[at]i.[et] Monachis de Colecestr' in escambiu[m] q[u]*a*ter viginti Ac[r]*a*rum t[er]re q[u]*a*s Will[elmus] pat[er] meus p[r]*i*us eisdem dona
uerat in parco suo de Takel[eia] i[n] pura[m].[et] p[er]petuam elemosinam. Hanc au[tem] donatione[m] feci p[ro] salute a[n]i[m]e d[omi]ni Regis Joh[ann]is.[et]
an[te]cessor[um].[et] successor[um] suor[um].[et] p[ro] salute a[n]i[m]e mee.[et] O[mn]i[u]m an[te]cessor[um].[et] h[er]edu[m] meor[um]. Et ego [et] h[er]edes mei warantizabim[us]
p[re]fatis Eccl[es]ie S[an]c[t]i Joh[ann]is.[et] Abb[at]i.[et] Monachis Colecestr' p[re]no[m]i[n]ata tenementa i[n] pura[m] [et] p[er]petuam elemosinam q[u]*i*etam ab Om[n]i
sec[u]lari seruitio.[et] exactione.[con]t[r]*a* Om[n]es ho[m]i[n]es.[et] fe[m]i[n]as. Hiis Testib[us]. Gaufr[ido] fil[io] pet[r]*i* Comite Esex'. Alb[r]*i*co de Ver Co
mite Oxon'. Will[elmo] fil[io] fulcon[is]. Rob[erto] de Cantelu. Rog[ero] de La Dune. Rad[ulfo] de Berners. Mag[ist]ro Rob[erto] de Cantia. Will[elmo]
de Haya. Alexand[ro] fil[io] Oseb[erni]. Ric[ardo] fil[io] pagani. Will[elmo] de Takel[eia]. Nich[olao] fil[io] Gerard[i]. Nigello de Hauekestun'. Ric[ardo] filio
Rad[ulfi]. Ric[ardo] de Bumsted'. Laure[n]t[io] de Takel[eia]. Reymundo de Selford'. Rog[ero] testard'. Rob[erto] de Campes. Rog[ero] de
teya. [Et] Multis Aliis;

Translation below.

[1] *Note dotted* y; *see also* Heynon, *Pl.*XX, *l.*4, Nassewyk, *Pl.*XXII, *l.*8. (*p.*1 *n.*11). *For another method, see p.*22 *n.*2, *and for abbreviation of the enclitic* -que, *see p.*1 *n.*10.

[2] *Note abbreviation of pronoun* q[u]e *by use of superior* e; *cf.* q[u]a (*p.*1 *n.*7) *and* q[u]i

Know [all men] present and to come that I, William de Hautville, son of William, have granted and given and by the present charter confirmed to the church of St. John the Baptist of Colchester and to the the abbot and monks of the same place, Ellis son of Gilbert and his whole tenement in Takeley, that is to say his messuage and three crofts of land which lie between the said messuage and the land of the church of Takeley, and one acre which lies between Le Wardbroc and between the land of Arnold Berard, and one acre of pasture which lies between the land of Arnold and the land of Hardwin, and the whole field from my demesne which is called Newenhale, with all their appurtenances in Takeley, except the mill situated in the same field, in pure and perpetual alms. And these aforesaid tenements I have given to the aforesaid abbot and monks of Colchester in exchange for eighty acres of land which William my father formerly gave them in his park of Takeley in pure and perpetual alms. This gift moreover I have made for the salvation of the soul of the Lord King, John, and of his ancestors and successors, and for the salvation of my soul and of all my ancestors and heirs. And I and my heirs will warrant to the aforesaid church of St. John and to the abbot and monks of Colchester, the beforenamed tenements in pure and perpetual alms, quit from all secular service and demand against all men and women. These being witnesses, Geoffrey son of Peter, Earl of Essex, Aubrey de Vere, Earl of Oxford, William son of Fulk, Robert de Cantelu, Roger de la Dune, Ralph de Berners, Master Robert of Kent, William de Haya, Alexander son of Osborn, Richard son of Payne, William of Takeley, Nicholas son of Gerard, Nigel de Hauekestun', Richard son of Ralph, Richard of Bumpstead, Laurence of Takeley, Raymond de Selford', Roger ' testard ', Robert of Camps, Roger of Tey, and many others.

EXCHANGE OF LAND, TAKELEY, *circa* 1212

William de Hautville exchanges a bondman and his holding, and part of the demesne, for 80 acres of land formerly granted to St. John's Abbey, Colchester, in frankalmoign, by his father William. The exchange must have taken place some time between the deaths of William, senior, *circa* 1211, and of Geoffrey, Earl of Essex, in 1213.

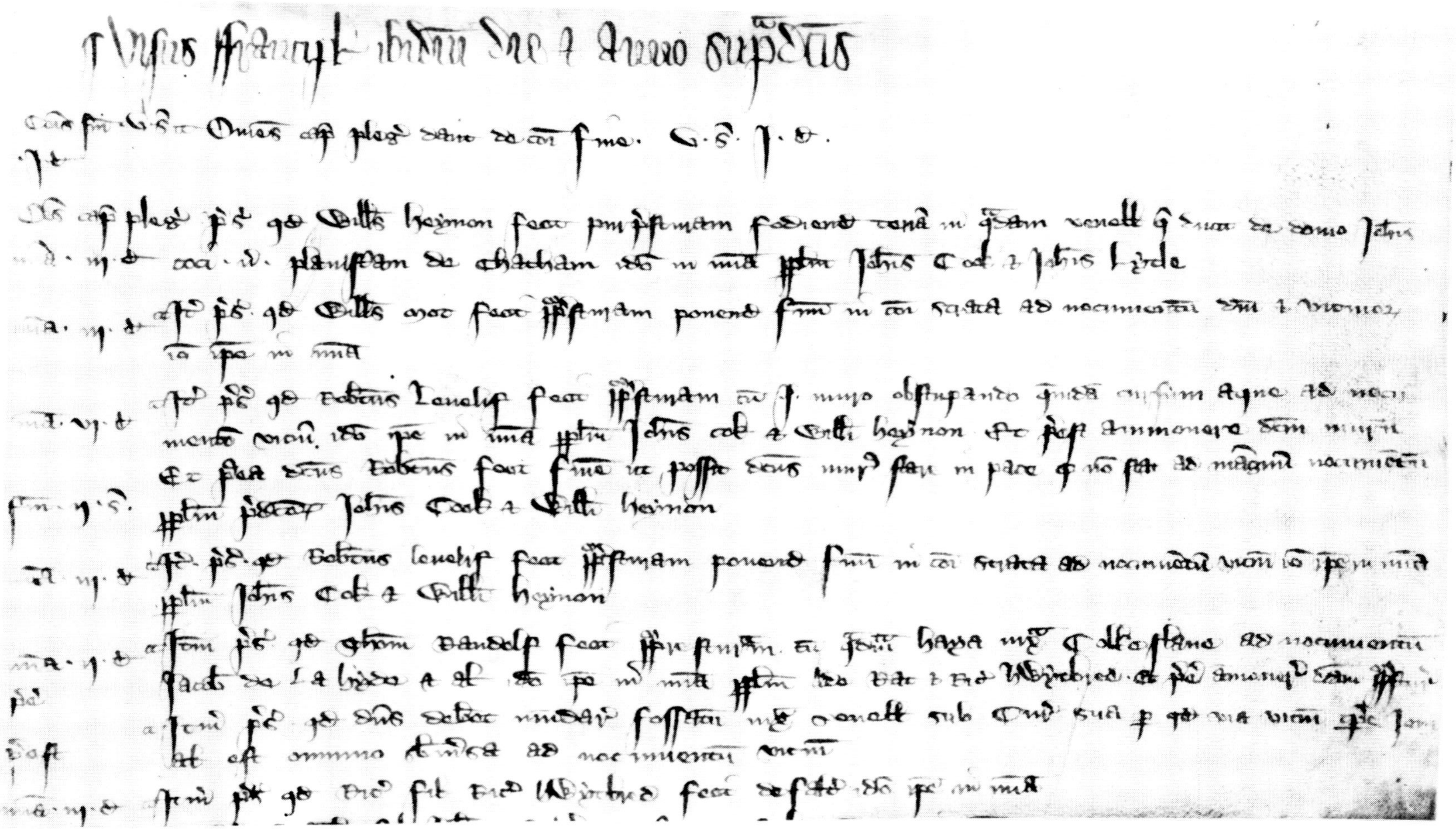

¶[1] Visus Francipl[egii] ibid[e]m die [et] anno sup[r]*a*d[i]c[t]is

Co[mmun]is fin[is] .v.s' .j.d' ¶Om[n]es cap[itales] pleg[ii] dant de co[mmun]i fine. v.s'. j.d'.

O[mn]es cap[itales] pleg[ii] p[re]s[entant] q[uo]d Will[elmu]s Heynon fecit purp[re]sturam fodiend[o] terra[m] in q[u]*a*dam venell[a] q[ue][2] ducit de domo Joh[ann]is coci.u[ersus]. planist[r]*i*am de Chatham id[e]o in mi[sericordi]a p[er]pl[egiu]m Joh[ann]is Cook [et] Joh[ann]is Lytle

mi[sericordi]a.iij.d'

mi[sericordi]a.iij.d' ¶It[em] p[re]s[entant]. q[uo]d Will[elmu]s Mot fecit p[ur]p[re]sturam ponend[o] fim[um] in co[mmun]i strata ad nocumentu[m] d[omi]ni [et] vicinor[um] i[de]o ip[s]e in mi[sericordi]a

mi[sericordi]a.vj.d' ¶It[em] p[re]s[entant] q[uo]d Rob[er]tus Leuelif fecit p[ur]p[re]sturam cu[m] .j. muro obstupando q[ue]mda[m] cursum aque ad nocumentu[m] vicin[orum] id[e]o ip[s]e in mi[sericordi]a p[er]pl[egiu]m Joh[ann]is cok [et] Will[elm]i Heynon. Et p[receptum] est ammouere d[i]c[tu]m muru[m]

fin[is].ij.s'. Et p[ost]ea[3] d[i]c[t]us Rob[er]tus fecit fine[m] ut possit d[i]c[t]us mur[us] stare in pace q[uia][4] no[n] stat ad ma[n]gnu[m] nocume[n]tu[m] p[er]pl[egiu]m p[re]d[i]c[t]or[um] Joh[ann]is Cook [et] Will[elm]i Heynon

mi[sericordi]a.iij.d' ¶It[em]. p[re]s[entant]. q[uo]d Rob[er]tus leuelif fecit p[ur]p[re]sturam ponend[o] fim[um] in co[mmun]i strata ad nocume[n]tu[m] vicin[orum] i[de]o ip[s]e in mi[sericordi]a p[er]pl[egiu]m Joh[ann]is Cok [et] Will[elm]i Heynon

mi[sericordi]a.ij.d' ¶It[em] p[re]s[entant]. q[uo]d Thom[as] Randolf fecit p[ur]prestur*a*m cu[m] q[u]*a*d*a*m Haya iux[t]*a* Colkeslane ad nocumentu[m] Jacob[i] de La Hyde [et] al[iorum] id[e]o ip[s]e in mi[sericordi]a p[er]pl[egiu]m Ade Rat [et] Ric[ardi] Hwytbred. Et p[receptum] e[st] a[m]mouer[e] d[i]c[t]am p[ur]p[re]stur[am]

p[receptum] e[st]

p[receptum] est ¶It[e]m p[re]s[entant]. q[uo]d d[omi]n[u]s deb[er]et mu[n]dar[e] fossatu[m] iux[t]*a* venell[am] sub Cur[ia] sua p[er] q[uo]d via vicin[a] t[em]p[or]e Iem al[i] est omnino s[u]bm[er]sa ad nocumentu[m] vicin[orum]

mi[sericordi]a.iij.d' ¶It[e]m p[re]s[entant] q[uo]d Ric[ardus] fil[ius] Ric[ardi] Hwytbred fecit defalt[am] id[e]o ip[s]e in mi[sericordi]a

Translation on p.31.

s' (s[olidi], shillings) *and* d' (d[enarii], pence) ***have not been extended in the transcript.***

[1] *Note paragraph mark; cf. another form, ll.2,6,8,12,14,16,18. See also Plates* XXI, XXII.

[2] *Note abbreviation of pronoun* q[ue]; *cf. p.21 n.2.*

[3] *Note use of special sign commonly denoting omission of* us (*see* mur[us], *same line, and p.1 n.13.) to abbreviate* p[ost]ea.

[4] *Note abbreviation of* q[uia]; *see also p.24 l.6.*

MANOR COURT ROLL, GREAT WALTHAM, 1318

Entries from the proceedings of the Court Leet of Walter de Mandeville, Lord of the Manor of Chatham Hall in Great Waltham. These entries are immediately preceded by those for the Court Baron.

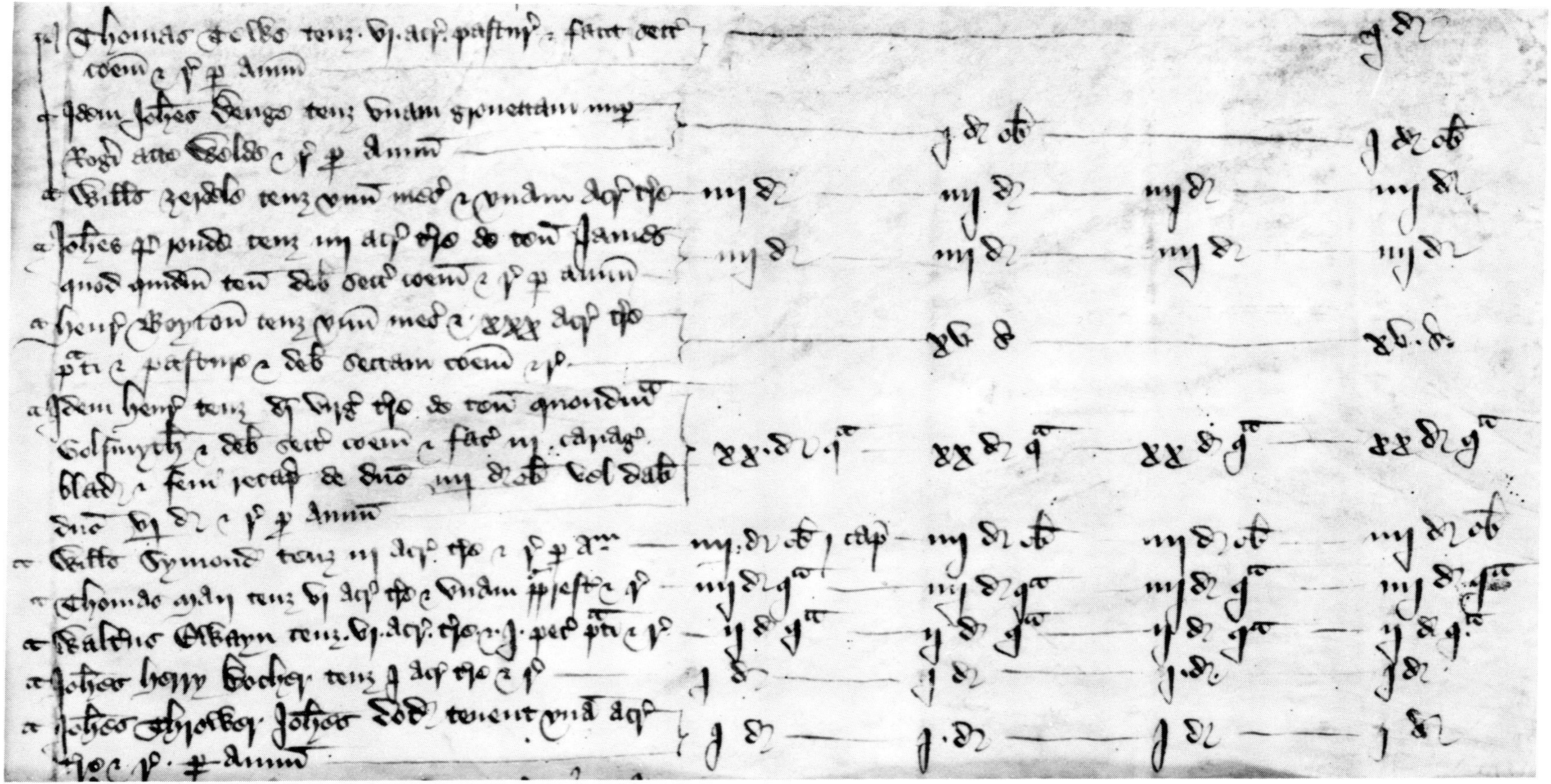

¶Thomas Tewe ten[et][1].vj.acr[as] pastur[e] [et] facit sect[am] co[mmun]em [et] r[eddit] p[er] annu[m]				j d'
¶Idem Joh[ann]es Benge ten[et] vnam grouettam nup[er] Rog[er]i atte Welde [et] r[eddit] p[er] annu[m]		j d' ob'		j d' ob'
¶Will[elmu]s Yerdele[2] ten[et] vnu[m] mes[uagium] [et] vnam acr[am] t[er]re	iiij d'	iiij d'	iiij d'	iiij d'
¶Joh[ann]es Proude ten[et] iiij acr[as] t[er]re de ten[emento] James quod quid[e]m ten[ementum] deb[et] sect[am] co[mmun]em [et] r[eddit] p[er] annu[m]	iiij d'	iiij d'	iiij d'	iiij d'
¶Henr[icus] Boyton' ten[et] vnu[m] mes[uagium] [et].xxx acr[as] t[er]re p[r]*ati* [et] pasture [et] deb[et] sectam co[mmun]em [et] r[eddit]		xv.s'		xv.s'.
¶Idem Henr[icus] ten[et] dj'[3] virg[atam] t[er]re de ten[emento] quond*am* Golsmyth' [et] deb[et] sect[am] co[mmun]em [et] fac[it] iij cariag[ia]. blad[i] [et] feni recap[iendo] de d[omi]no iiij d' ob' vel dab[it] d[omi]no vj d' [et] r[eddit] p[er] annu[m]	xx.d' qª	xx d' qª	xx d' qª	xx d' qª
¶Will[elmu]s Symond' ten[et] iij acr[as] t[er]re [et] r[eddit] p[er] a[nnu]*m*	iiij.d' ob' j cap[onem]	iiij d' ob'	iiij d' ob'	iiij d' ob'
¶Thomas Maij ten[et] vj acr[as] t[er]re [et] vnam p[ur]prest[uram] [et] r[eddit]	iiij d' qª	iiij d' qª	iiij d' qª	iiij d' qª.
¶Walt[er]us Ewayn ten[et].vj.acr[as].t[er]re.[et].j. pec[iam] p[r]*ati* [et] r[eddit]	ij d' qª	ij d' qª	ij d' qª	ij d' qª.
¶Joh[ann]es Herry Bocher ten[et] j acr[am] t[er]re [et] r[eddit]	j d'	j d'	j.d'.	j d'
¶Joh[ann]es Thrower Joh[ann]es dod' tenent vna[m] acr[am] t[er]re [et]. r[eddunt]. p[er] annu[m]	j d'	j.d'	j d'	j d'

Translation on p.32.

s', d', ob' (ob[olus], halfpenny) *and* qª (q[uart]*a*, farthing) *have not been extended in the transcript.*

[1] *Note use of special sign for* et *described on p.1 n.10; see also p.26 n.1.*

[2] *Note letter resembling written* z (' yogh '), *descended from flat-headed Anglo-Saxon* g, *and printed here as now pronounced,* Y; *cf. p.4 n.8. This name developed into Yardley; other forms of it found in the Middle Ages in Thaxted are* Gerdelai, Girdele, Jerdelle.

[3] di[midiam].

EXTRACT FROM MANORIAL SURVEY, THAXTED, *circa* 1395

This extract from an exhaustive survey roll, over 28 feet long, of the Manor of Thaxted with the Borough, includes the names of some of the ' forensic ' freehold tenants, that is, those who lived outside the town, as distinct from the ' burgenses '. The four columns show the payments due each quarter, at Christmas, Easter, the Nativity of St. John the Baptist, and Michaelmas.

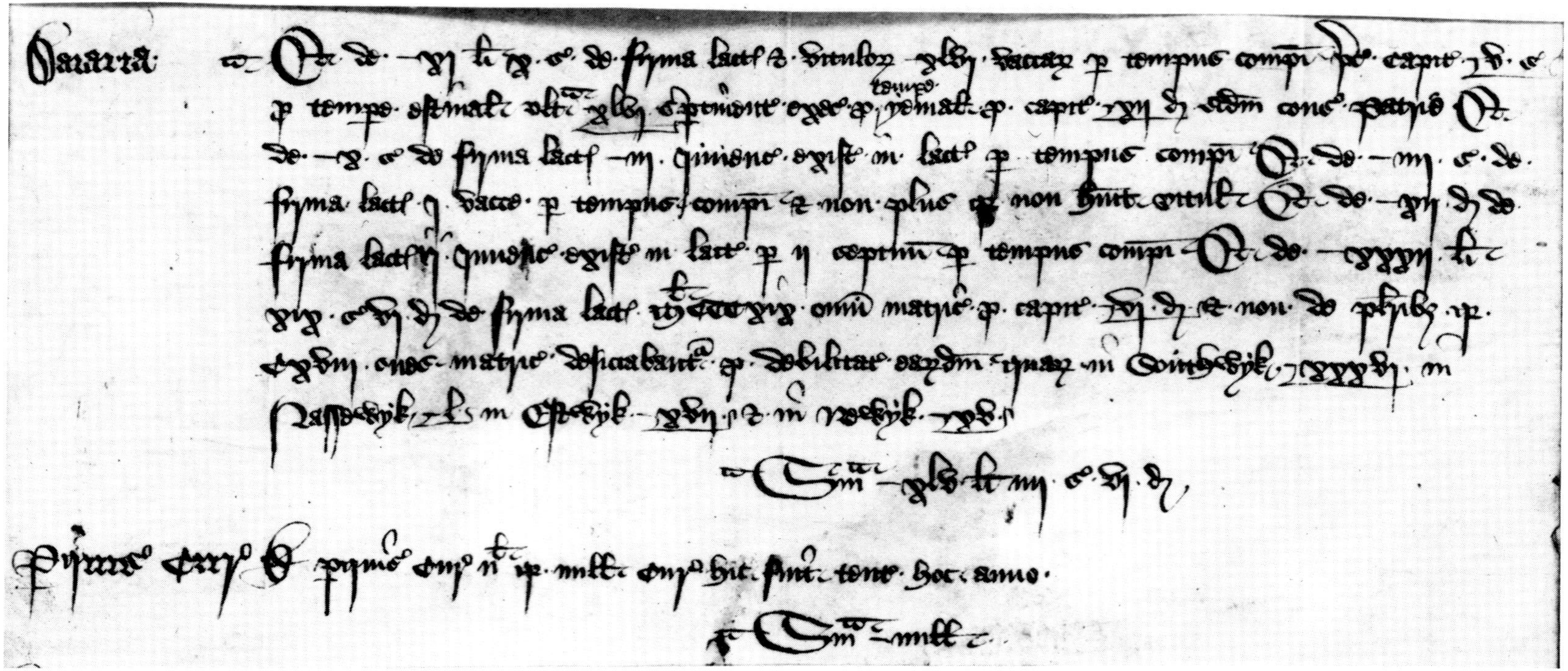

Daiaria.

¶Et de. —xj li' x.s'. de.firma lact[is][1] [et].vitulor[um] —xlvj.vaccar[um].p[er] tempus comp[ot]i p[re]c[io].Capit[is][2]. v.s' p[ro] temp[or]e.estiual[i] vlt[r]*a* xlvj s' p[er]tinent[es].exec[utoribus].p[ro].temp[or]e[3].yemal[i].p[ro].capit[e]. xij d' s[e]c[un]d[u]m cons[uetudinem].Patrie Et de. —x.s' de firma lact[is] —iij. Juuenc[arum].exist[entium].in.lact[e] p[er] tempus comp[ot]i Et de. —iiij.s'. de. firma lact[is].j. vacce.p[er] tempus comp[ot]i [et].non.plus q[uia] non h[ab]uit vitul[um] Et de. —xij.d' de. firma lact[is] ij. Juuenc[arum].exist[entium] in lact[e]. p[er] ij septim[anas] p[er] tempus comp[ot]i Et de. —xxxij.li' xix.s' vj.d' de firma lact[is]. Ml'CCCxix.ouiu[m] matric[um].p[ro].capit[e]. vj.d'. [et].non.de pl[u]rib[us].q[uia]. Cxviij.oues.matric[es].deficiabant[ur].p[ro].debilitat[e].ear[un]d[e]m[4].quar[um] in Southwyk.xxxvj. in Nassewyk l. in Estwyk.xvij. [et].in Newyk.xv.

¶S[um]m*a*—xlv.li' iiij.s'. vj.d'

P[er]quis[ita] Cu· [ie]

D[e][5] p[er]quis[itis] Cur[ie] n[ihi]*l*[6] q[uia].null[a] Cur[ia] hic fuit tent[a].hoc anno.

¶S[um]m*a* —null[um]

Translation below.

Slightly reduced.

li' (li[bre], pounds), s' *and* d' *have not been extended in the transcript.* lact', *extended as* lact[is], *might be better extended throughout* lact[agii]; *the phrase has been noted in some other compoti in the form* de firma lactag' et vitulorum; *if so the translation would be* by rent of dairy produce and calves.

1 *Note form of suspension after final* t; *see p.2 n.1.*

2 *Note another form of suspension after final* t, *a variation of the sign described on p.1 n.6, a little hook up on the last stroke of the final letter; it is also used in this example with final* c, r *and* s.

3 temp[or]e *interlined. Note horizontal stroke through descender of* p *here denoting* p[or]; *cf. p.1 n.5 for more usual significance. For another example of this usage, see p.22 l.16.*

4 *Note special sign described on p.1 n.8 used medially to abbreviate* ear[un]dem; *see next word* quar[um] *for its more common use.*

5 *Note abbreviation of* D[e].

6 *Note abbreviation of* n[ihi]*l*.

Dairy

And for £11.10s. by rent of milk and calves of 46 cows for the time of the account at 5s. per head for the summertime, besides[ ]46s. belonging to the officers for the wintertime at 12d. per head according to the custom of the country. And for 10s. by rent of milk of three cows being in milk for the time of the account. And for 4s. by rent of milk of 1 cow for the time of the account and not more because it had no calf. And for 12d. by rent of milk of 2 cows in milk for 2 weeks during the time of the account. And for £32. 19s. 6d. by rent of milk of 1319 mother ewes at 6d. per head and not for more because 118 mother ewes are short because of the sickness of the same of which 36 are in Southwyk, 50 in Nassewyk, 17 in Estwyk, and 15 in Newyk.

Total —£45. 4s. 6d.

Perquisites of the Court

From perquisites of the court nothing because no court was held here this year.

Total —nothing.

EXTRACT FROM MANORIAL COMPOTUS, FOULNESS, 1425

The Essex coastal marshlands and islands, such as Foulness, carried large flocks of sheep, of whose milk cheeses were made. The dairy sheds were known as ' wickes '. Norden in 1594 described the Hundred of Rochford, in which Foulness lay, as yielding ' milke, butter and cheese in admirable aboundance ' The Foulness manorial accounts reflect this feature of the local economy.

PLATE XXIII

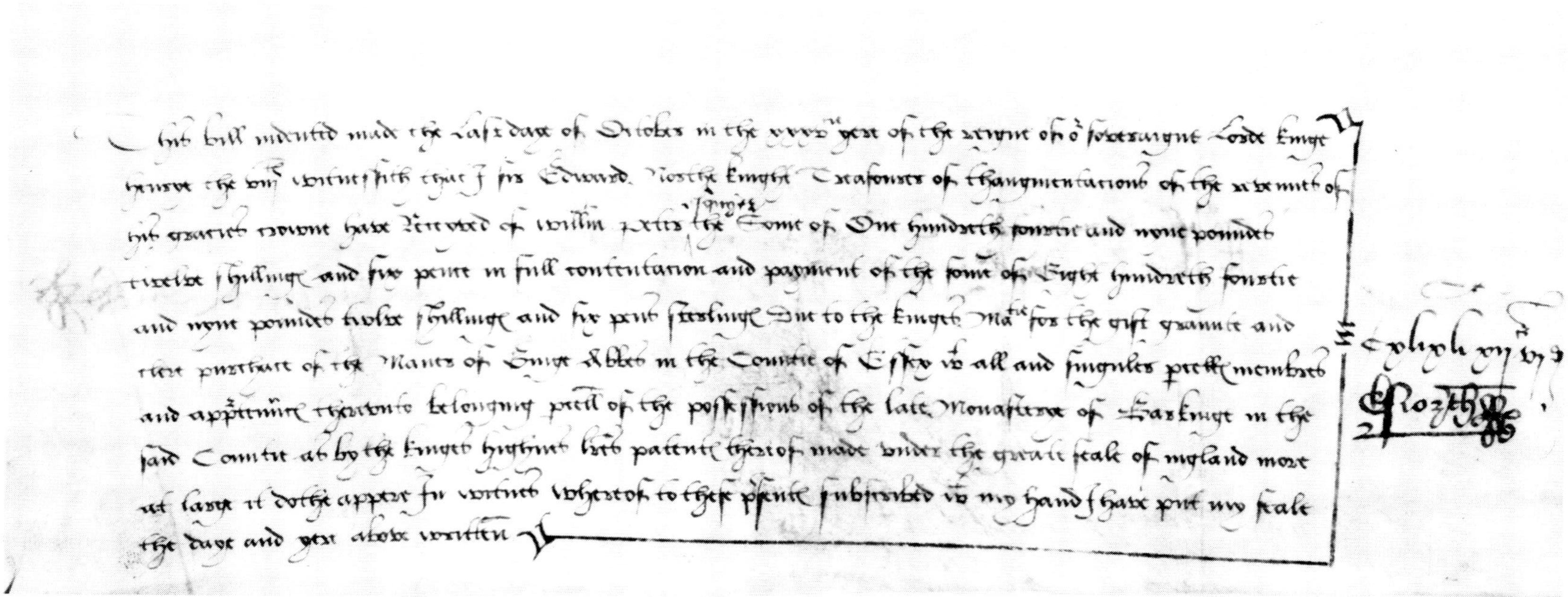
This bill indented made the last daye of October in the xxxv^th yere of the reigne of o^r soveraigne Lorde Kinge
Henrye the viii^th witnessith that I Sir Edward Northe knight Treasourer of thaugmentacions of the revenues of
his graces crowne have receyved of Willm Petre knight the some of One hundreth fourtie and nyne poundes
twelve shillinges and fyve pence in full contentacion and payment of the some of Eight hundreth fourtie
and nyne poundes twelve shillinges and fyve pens sterlinge due to the Kinges Matie for the gift graunte and
clere purchace of the Manor of Ginge Abbes in the Countie of Essex with all and singuler their members
and appurtenaunces thereunto belonginge parcell of the possessions of the late Monasterie of Barkinge in the
said Countie as by the Kinges highnes lettres patentes thereof made under the greate seale of England more
at large it dothe apper In witnes whereof to these presentes subscribed with my hand I have put my seale
the daye and yere above written

cxlix li xii s v d
Northe

This bill indented made the Last daye of October in the xxxv^{tie}[1] yere of the reigne of o^{r} soveraigne Lorde kinge henrye the viijth' witnessith that I sir Edward Northe knight Treasourer of thaugmentacions[2] of the revenues of his gracies crowne have Receyved of Will[ia]m Peter esquyer[3] the Some of One hundreth fourtie and nyne poundes twelve shilling[es] and six pence in full contentacion and payment of the some of Eight hundreth fourtie and nyne poundes twlve[4] shilling[es] and six pens sterling[es] due to the kinges Matie for the gift graunte and clere purchace of the Maner of Ginge Abbes in the Countie of Essex w^{t} all and singuler p[ar]cell[es] membres and app[u]rtena[u]nc[es] therevnto belonging p[ar]cell' of the possessions of the late Monasterye of Barkinge in the said Countie as by the kinges highnes l[ett]res[5] patent[es] thereof made vnder the greate seale of ingland more at large it dothe appere In witnes whereof to these p[re]sent[es] subscribed w^{t} my hand I have put my seale the daye and yere above written'——————

Cxlix li' xij^{s}' vj d'
E North'[6]

li', s' *and* d' *have not been extended in the transcript.*

[1] *i.e.* five and thirtie.

[2] *Note elision of* e *of definite article, a fairly common practice in English documents of the 16th and 17th centuries.*

[3] esquyer *interlined.*

[4] *Sic in MS.*

[5] *For this extension, cf.* membres, *l.*6, *and p.*8 *n.*5. *See also the heading in full,* Small Lettres, *on p.*40 *of de Beauchesne and Baildon,* A Booke Containing Divers Sortes of Hands, 1571.

[6] *Note ' paraph ', a distinctive kind of decorative flourishing associated with personal signatures, often produced by elaboration of the underlining.*

INDENTED BILL OF RECEIPT, INGATESTONE, 1543

A neatly-written example of the Secretary Hand (*see* Fig. 1). The wavy line of the indenture can be seen faintly at the top. The Manor of Ingatestone had formed part of the estates of Barking Abbey. Barely a month after the surrender of the Abbey William Petre bought the manor for £849. 12. 6. This receipt acknowledges payment of the final instalment of the purchase money five years later.

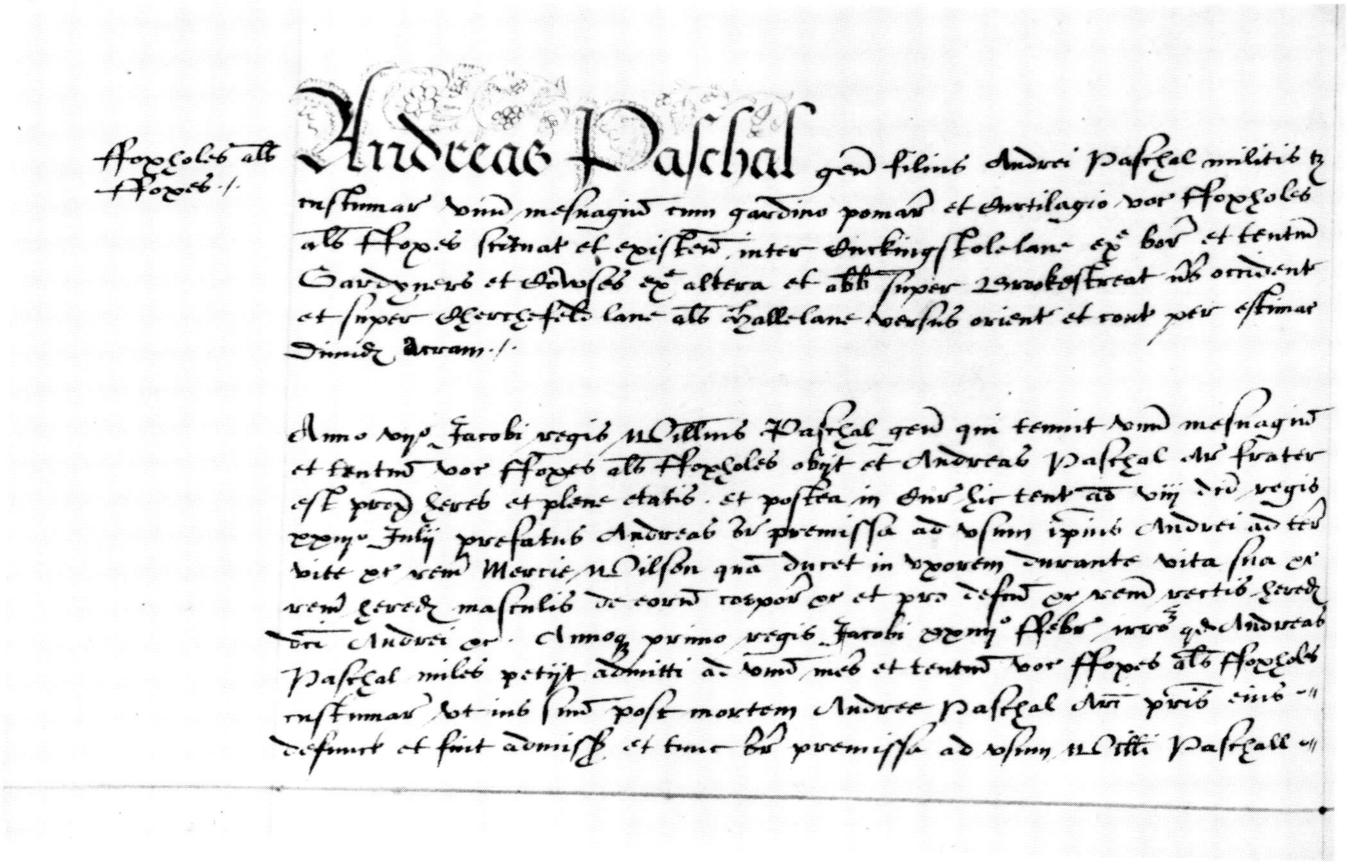

Foxholes al[ia]s Foxes./.

Andreas Paschal gen[erosus] filius Andrei Paschal militis t[enet][1] custumar[ie] vnu[m] mesuagiu[m] cum gardino pomar[io] et Curtilagio voc[atum] Foxholes al[ia]s Foxes scituat[um] et existen[s] inter Cuckingstolelane ex[part]*e* bor[eali] et ten[emen]t[u]m Gardyners et Cowses ex[part]*e* altera et abb[uttat] super Brookestreat u[er]s[us] occident[em] et super Cherchefeld lane al[ia]s Hallelane versus orient[em] et cont[inet] per estimac[ionem] dimid[iam] acram./.

Anno vij° Jacobi regis Will[el]m[u]s Paschal gen[erosus] qui tenuit vnu[m] mesuagiu[m] et ten[emen]t[u]m voc[atum] Foxes al[ia]s Foxholes obijt et Andreas Paschal Ar[miger] frater est prox[imus] heres et plene etatis. et postea in Cur[ia] hic tent[a] a[nn]o viij d[i]c[t]i regis xxiij° Julij prefatus Andreas s[ursum]r[eddidit][2] premissa ad vsum ip[s]ius Andrei ad ter[minum] vite &c' rem[anentia] Mercie Wilson qua[m] ducet in vxorem durante vita sua &c' rem[anentia] hered[ibus] masculis de eoru[m] corpor[ibus] &c' et pro def[e]c[t]u &c' rem[anentia] rectis hered[ibus] d[i]c[t]i Andrei &c'. Annoq[ue] primo regis Jacobi xxiiij° Febr[uarij] irro[tulatu]*r* q[uo]d Andreas Paschal miles petijt admitti ad vnu[m] mes[uagium] et ten[emen]t[u]m voc[atum] Foxes al[ia]s Foxholes custumar[ium] vt ius suu[m] post mortem Andree Paschal Ar[miger]i p[at]ris eius [3] defunct[i] et fuit admiss[us] et tunc s[ursum]r[eddidit] premissa ad vsum Will[elm]i Paschall

Translation below.

[1] *Note use of special sign described on p.1 n.10; it is more strictly used to abbreviate the* ***same word on p.23 l.1.***

[2] *Note extreme abbreviation of common manorial form; cf. p.22 l.15* ,p'e '(p[receptum] e[st]).

[3] *Note space-fillers at end of this and next line.*

Foxholes, otherwise Foxes

Andrew Paschal, gentleman, son of Andrew Paschal, knight, holds customarily one messuage, with garden, orchard and yard, called Foxholes, otherwise Foxes, situated and being between Cuckingstolelane on the north part and the tenement, Gardyners and Cowses, on the other part, and it abuts on Brookstreat towards the west and on Cherchefeld Lane, otherwise Hallelane towards the east, and it contains by estimation half an acre.

In the seventh year of King James William Paschal, gentleman, who held one messuage and tenement called Foxes, otherwise Foxholes, died, and Andrew Paschal, esquire, his brother, is his next heir and of full age. And afterwards in the Court held here in the eighth year of the said king on the 23rd July the aforesaid Andrew surrendered the premises to the use of Andrew himself to the end of his life etc., the remainder to Mercy Wilson whom he shall take (*sic*) to wife, for her lifetime etc., the remainder to the heirs male of their bodies etc., and in default of etc., the remainder to the right heirs of the said Andrew etc. And in the first year of King James on the 24th February it is enrolled that Andrew Paschal, knight, sought to be admitted to one customary messuage and tenement called Foxes, otherwise Foxholes, as his right after the death of Andrew Paschal, esquire, his father, deceased, and was admitted and then surrendered the premises to the use of William Paschall.

EXTRACT FROM MANORIAL SURVEY, GREAT BADDOW, 1605

Some manorial surveys not only describe in precise terms the situation and tenure of properties, but, like this one, trace their previous ownership by reference to court rolls and rentals. Sometimes they quote from documents no longer extant. Cuckingstole Lane was subsequently, and till recently, known as Sluts Lane.

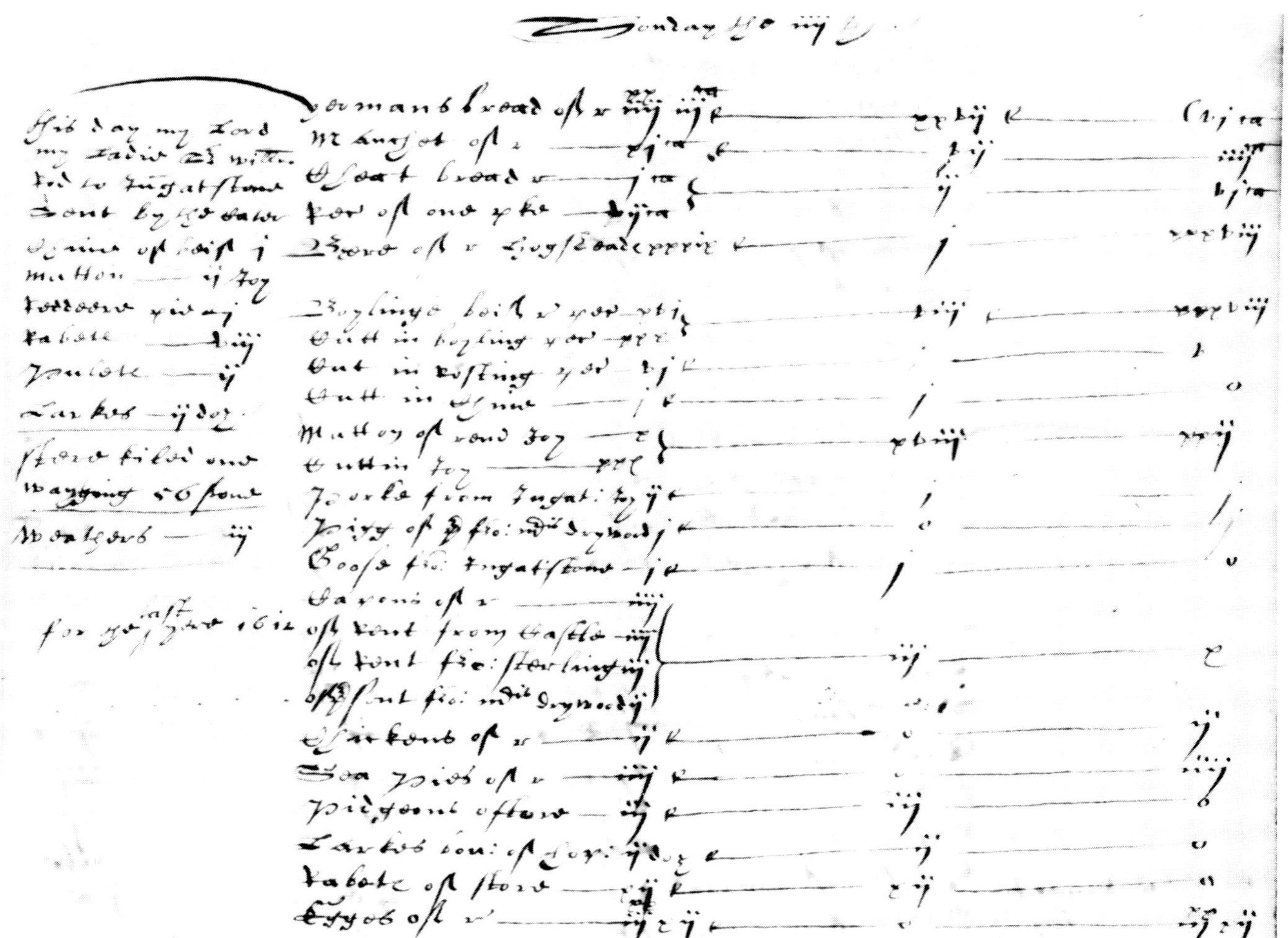

Monday the iij ...

This day my Lord
my Ladie and ...
red to Ingatstone
sent by the carte
A grine of beif j
mutton — ij qr
[illegible]
Rabets — iiij
Pullets — ij
Larkes — ij doz
Steere kild one
wayeing 56 stone
Wheateres — iij

for the last yeare 1612

Yeomans bread of r
Manchet of r
Cheat bread r
... of one ...
Beere of r hogsheade xxxix
Boylinge beif r ...
Mutt in boyling ...
Mutt in rosting ...
Mutt in Chine
Mutton of rend qr
Mutton qr
Porke from Ingat:
Pigg of ... fro: Mrs Drywood
Goose fro: Ingatstone
Capons of r
of rent from Castle
of rent fro: Sterling
of rent fro: Mrs Drywood
Chickens of r
Sea pies of r
Pigeons of store
Larkes bou: of store ij doz
Rabets of store
Egges of r

Sonday the iiijth./

this day my Lord	Yeomans bread of r[emainder]	iiij^{xx} iij$^{ca[st]}$[1]	xxvij	lvj ca[st]
my Ladie Sr Will[ia]m	Manchet of r	xj^{ca}	vij	iiij^{ca}
Rod to Ingatstone[2]	Cheat bread r	j ca }	ij	vj ca
Sent by the Cater	Rec' of one p[ec]ke	vij ca }		
Chine of beif j	Beere of r Hogshead[es]	xxxix	j	xxxviij
Mutton——ij Joy[ntes]				
Reddeere pie —j	Boylinge beif r' pec[es]	xvj }	viij	xxxviij
Rabet[es]———viij	Cutt in boyling pec'	xxx }		
Pulet[es]———ij	Cut in Rosting pec'	vj	j	v
Larkes—ij doz./	Cutt in Chine	j	j	o
	Mutton of rem' Joy[ntes]	x }	xviij	xxij
stere kiled one	Cutt in Joy[ntes]	xxx }		
wayging[3] 56 stone	Porke from Ingat: Joy[ntes]	ij	j	j
Weathers———iij	Pigg of p[resent] fro: m^{ris} drywood	j	o	j
	Goose fro: Ingatstone	j	j	o
	Capons of r	iiij }		
for the last[4] yere 1612	of Rent from Castle	iiij }		
	of Rent fro: sterling	iij }	iij	x
. . . . .	of p[re]sent fro: m^{ris} drywood	ij }		
	Chickens of r	ij	o	ij
	Sea Pies of r	iiij	o	iiij
	Pidgeons oftore[5]	iij	iij	o
	Larkes bou[ght] of hop[trough][6]	ij doz	ij	o
	Rabet[es] of store	xij	xij	o
	Egges of r'	iij^{xx}xij	o	iij^{xx}xij

[1] *i.e.* Fourscore and three (83) cast; *cf. W. Harrison*, Description of England, 1587 *quoted* Oxford English Dictionary): Of the flower of one bushell . . . they make fortie cast of manchet.

[2] *Note superfluous abbreviation stroke. See also p.3 n.4.*

[3] *Sic in MS.*

[4] last *interlined.*

[5] *Sic in MS.*; *recte* of store.

[6] *Extension of name confirmed elsewhere in account.*

HOUSEHOLD ACCOUNTS, WEST HORNDON, 1612

John, Lord Petre, son of Sir William Petre, used Thorndon Hall, West Horndon, as his principal seat, visiting Ingatestone Hall from time to time. The marginal notes in the accounts are of provisions sent over to Ingatestone from West Horndon on the occasion of such a visit. 'Thexpencis of my Lordes houshold at Westhorndon' were entered up daily and weekly in meticulous detail. The entry above is for one day in October. The first column of quantities shows the stock of provisions at the beginning of the day (e.g. Cheat bread, 1 cast left over from the day before, and 7 cast new-baked from 1 peck of flour, 8 cast in all); the second column shows the quantity consumed during the day; the third column shows the remainder at the end of the day, to be carried forward and entered in the first column for the next day, with any fresh provisions received. On Saturday the week's consumption was costed in detail, differentiating between provisions 'of store' (including estate produce, rents in kind, and gifts), and provisions 'bought'.

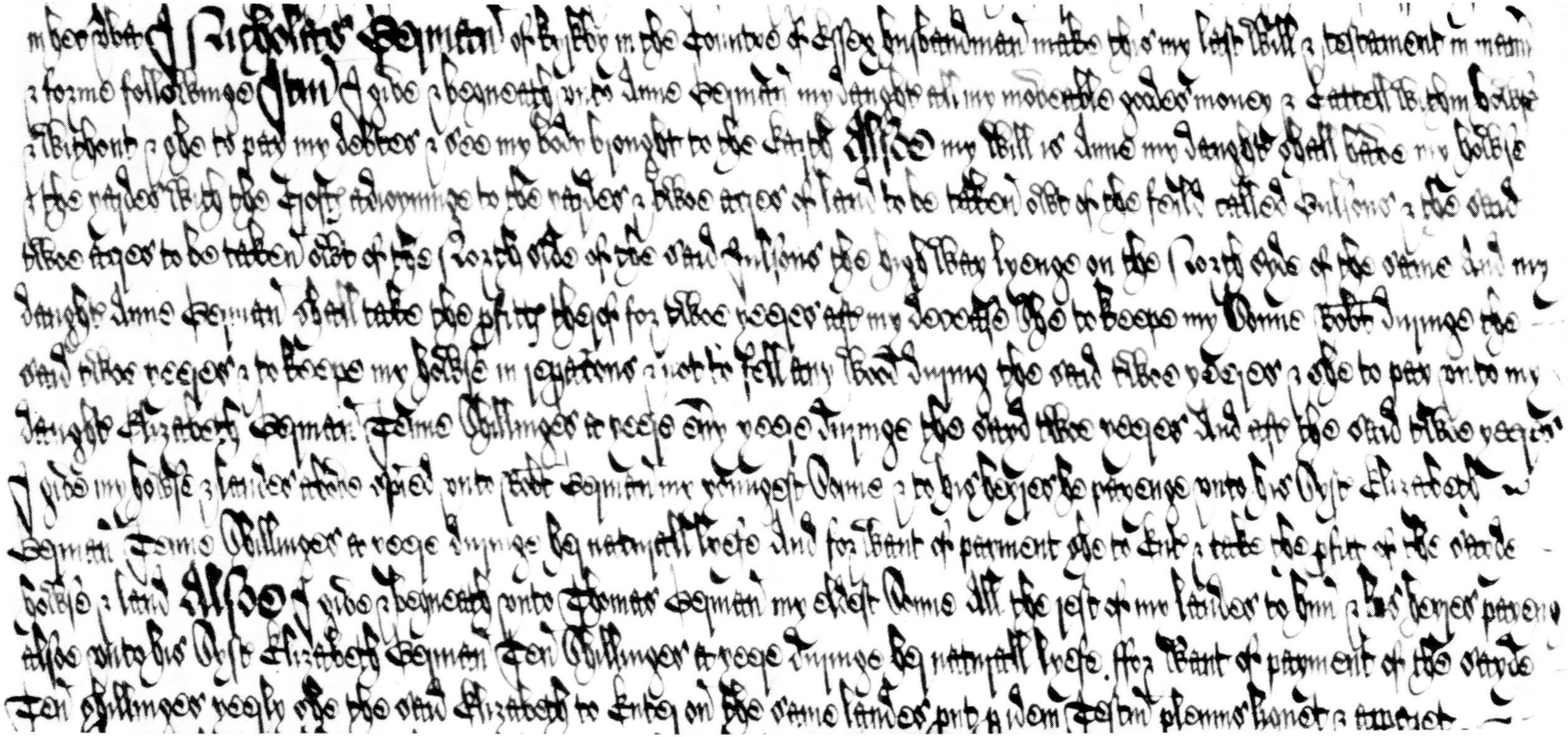
[illegible] I Nicholas Seyman of Ryssby in the countie of Essex husbandman make this my last will & testament in maner & forme followinge Item I give & bequeath unto Anne Seyman my daughter all my moveable goodes money & cattell which being [illegible] & she to pay my debtes & see my body brought to the church Also my will is Anne my daughter shall have my house & the [illegible] to the [illegible] adjoyninge to the [illegible] & five acres of land to be taken out of the field called [illegible] & the said five acres to be taken out of the North side of the said [illegible] the highway lyenge on the North side of the same And my daughter Anne Seyman shall take the profitt thereof for five yeres after my decease she to keepe my sonne Robert dyringe the said five yeres & to keepe my house in reparations & not to fell any wood dyring the said five yeres & she to pay unto my daughter Elizabeth Seyman Tenne shillinges a yere every yere dyringe the said five yeres And after the said five yeres I give my house & landes above said unto Robert Seyman my youngest sonne & to his heires he payenge unto his sister Elizabeth Seyman Tenne shillinges a yere dyringe her naturall lyfe And for want of payment she to entre & take the profitt of the said house & land Also I give & bequeath unto Thomas Seyman my eldest sonne all the rest of my landes to him & his heires payeng also unto his sister Elizabeth Seyman Ten shillinges a yere dyringe her naturall lyfe. ffor want of payment of the said Ten shillinges yearly she the said Elizabeth to entre on the same landes [illegible] plenius liquet & [illegible]

in hec v[er]ba **I Nicholas German'** of kyrkby in the Countye of Essex husbandman' make this my last will & testament in mann[er] & forme followinge **It[e]m** I give & bequeath vnto Anne German' my daught[er][1] all my moveable goodes money & Cattell within howse & without & she to pay my debtes & see my body brought to the Earth **Alsoe** my will is Anne my daught[er] shall have my howse & the yardes with the Croft[es] adioyninge to the yardes & twoe acres of land to be taken' owt of the feild called Gulsons & the said twoe acres to be taken' owt of the North side of the said Julsons the highway lyenge on the North syde of the same And my daught[er] Anne German' shall take the p[ro]fitt[es] therof for twoe yeeres aft[er] my decease She to keepe my Sonne Rob[er]t duringe the said twoe yeeres & to keepe my howse in rep[ar]ac[i]ons & not to fell any wood during the said twoe yeeres & she to pay vnto my daught[er] Elizabeth German' Tenne Shillinges a yeere eu[er]y yeere duringe the sayd twoe yeeres And aft[er] the said twoe yeeres I give my howse & landes above sp[ecif]ied vnto Rob[er]t German' my youngest Sonne & to his heyres he payenge vnto his Syst[er] Elizabeth German' Tenne Shillinges a yeere duringe her naturall lyefe And for want of payment she to Ent[er] & take the p[ro]fitt of the sayde howse & land **Alsoe** I give & bequeath vnto Thomas German' my eldest Sonne All the rest of my landes to him & his heyres payeng alsoe vnto his Syst[er] Elizabeth German' Ten' Shillinges a yeere duringe her naturall lyefe For want of payment of the sayde Ten' shillinges yeerly she the said Elizabeth to Enter on' the same landes p[ro]ut p[er] idem Test[amentu]m plenius liquet [et] apparet

This is a typical example of the Legal Hand frequently encountered in local archives of the 16*th and* 17*th centuries in manor court rolls, title deeds, and the more formal documents of the Court of Quarter Sessions, such as indictments. Note unneccessary flourishes above line after final* n *throughout. See note on this practice on p.*ii.

[1] *See p.*24 *n.*2; *see also* aft[er] (*l.*6), Ent[er] (*l.*10), Syst[er] (*l.*12).

ENROLLED WILL, KIRBY-LE-SOKEN, 1613

A manorial tenant could not devise a copyhold estate by will; he had to surrender the property to the use of his will, and then declare his intent in his will; the property passed not by the will, but by the surrender. Among other matters brought before the Manor Court of Kirby-le-Soken, the homage presented that Nicholas German, who held certain properties at the will of the lord according to the custom of the manor, on his deathbed, before witnesses, had surrendered these properties to the use of his will. His children, Thomas, Robert and Anne, appeared and produced the above will, proved in the Commissary Court of the Soken, and Anne was admitted in accordance with its provisions. The will was enrolled with the proceedings of the court.

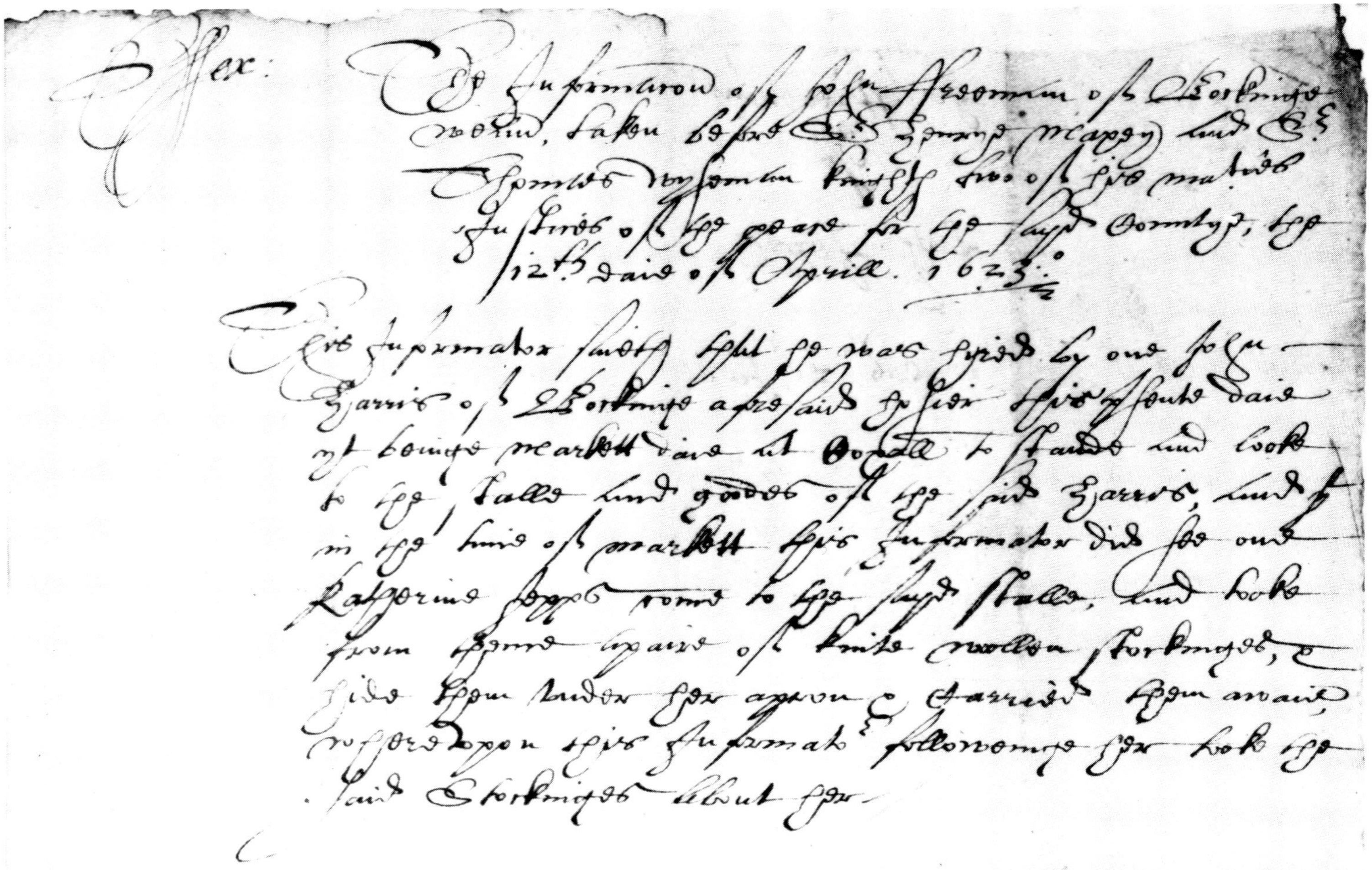

Essex: The Informacion of John Freeman of Bockinge weaver, taken before Sr Henry Maxey and Sr Thomas Wiseman knightes two of his maties Justices of the peace for the saied County, the 12th daie of Aprill. 1623.

This Informator saieth that he was hiered by one John Harris of Bockinge aforesaid the[?] this present daie yt beinge markett daie at Coxall[?] to stande and looke to the stalle and goodes of the said Harris, and in the tyme of markett this Informator did see one Katherine Jepps[?] come to the sayd stalle, and toke from thence a paire of knite wollen stockinges, & hide them under her apron & carried them awaie, whereupon this Informator followinge her toke the said Stockinges about her-

Essex: The Informac[i]on[1] of John Freeman of Bockinge weau[er], taken before S^r^. Henrye Maxey and S^r^. Thomas[2] Wyseman knight[es] two of his ma^ties^. Justices of the peace for the sayd Countye, the 12th. daie of Aprill. 1623:^o^ [3]

This Informator saieth that he was hired by one John —— Harris of Bockinge aforesaid hosier this p[re]sente daie yt[4] beinge markett daie at Coxall' to stande and looke to the stalle and goodes of the said Harris, and y^t^ [5] in the time of markett this Informator did see one Katherine Jepps come to the sayd stalle, and tooke from thence apaire of knite woollen stockinges, & hide them vnder her apron & Carried them awaie, wherevpon this Informato^r^ followeinge her tooke the said Stockinges about her./

[1] *Note omission of* i *in ending* -cion. *See also p.*28 *l.*7 *and note on p.*ii.
[2] *Note awkward appearance of* a *followed by* s, *almost suggesting an* e; *see also* was, *l.*6. *The form of this* s *can be seen clearly in* Harris, *l.*9, *and* this, *ll.*10, 14.
[3] *i.e.* Millesimo sescentesimo vicesimo tercio.
[4] *Here* y *stands for* i; *cf. n.*5.
[5] *Here* y *stands for* th, *i.e.* [th] [a]*t*; *see p.*7 *n.*3.

DEPOSITION TAKEN BY JUSTICES OF THE PEACE, 1623

One of the duties of Justices out of Sessions was to examine persons brought before them suspected of felony, and to take down the information against them. From the Quarter Sessions Rolls it appears that Katherine Jepps, accused above, was indicted for stealing the stockings, valued at 8d., at the following Easter Sessions on 24th April. She and her sureties failed to appear, and the recognizance was estreated.

In the Chamber over ye Kitchen

Inprimis the Chymney side of the roome hanged wth Twoe peeces of very old Tapestry Hanginges. A longe Thicke planke for a Table lynge upon Twoe Tressles, A ioynd stoole, Twoe buffitt Stooles, A Cushion Case of Needleworke, a payre of playinge Tables of Ivory & Ebony wth a sett of Men of the same in a Case of blacke Leather, A Standinge Bedstead wth turnd posts wth the Testerne head & Vallence of blacke Velvett & white Cloath of Sylver paned, the Vallence havinge a deepe fringe of blacke & white Silke in partes, the bed corded on the Bottome, A Bedmatt, A featherbedd & Bolster of Tike matiged, And old Tike pillowe, Twoe wollen homespum Blanketts wth Seames in the middest, Another wollen Blankett A portable Bedstead lynge in one of the presses, A square Baskett of Wicker whereim to carry plate, Three Wicker Flasketts, A Threesquare ioynd stoole, a fireshovell A payre of Tonges, A paire of Bellowes And Twoe old Windowe Curtaines of redd & greene Say with a Curtaine rodd — 05 00 00

Item a greate Base Violl — 00 14 00

In the Chamber over ye Kitchen./

Inpr[imis] the Chymney side of the roome hanged wth Twoe peeces[1] of very old Tapestry Hanginges, A longe Thicke planke for a Table lyinge vpon Twoe Tressles, A ioynd stoole, Twoe buffitt Stooles, A Cushion Case of Needleworke, a payre of playinge Tables of Ivory & Ebony wth a sett of Men of the same in a Case of blacke Leather, A standinge Bedstead wth turnd posts wth the Testerne head & Vallence of blacke Veluett & white Cloath of syluer paued[2], the Vallence havinge a deepe fringe of blacke & white Silke in partes, the Bed corded on the Bottome, A Bedmatt, A featherbedd & Bolster of Tike matched, An old Tike pillowe, Twoe woollen homespunn Blanketts wth Seames in the middest, Another woollen blankett, A portable Bedstead lyinge in one of the presses, A square Baskett of Wickar wherein to carry plate, Three Wickar Flasketts, A Threesquare ioynd stoole, a fireshovell, A payre of Tonges, A paire of Bellowes And Twoe old Windowe Curtaines of redd & greene Say with a Curtaine rodd	05 00 00[3]
It[e]m a greate Base Violl	00 15 00

For definition of terms used in household inventories, see Oxford English Dictionary *and F. W. Steer,* Farm and Cottage Inventories of Mid-Essex, 1635-1749 (*Essex Record Office,* 1950).

[1] *Note here, and throughout, use of vertical looped stroke described on p.2 n.1, as final s; see note on p.* ii.

[2] *Sic;* paned *must have been intended*

[3] *Pounds, shillings and pence.*

EXTRACT FROM INVENTORY OF GOODS OF ROBERT, LORD PETRE, 1638

Robert, 3rd Lord Petre, died in October, 1638. An inventory of his goods was prepared after his death by his house-steward, Richard Chenery, gentleman. It included goods at Thorndon Hall, Ingatestone Hall, and at his house in Aldersgate Street, London, with additional details of mortgages, ready money, horses and cattle. The extract relates to a room in Ingatestone Hall.

TRANSLATIONS

Manor Court Roll, Great Waltham, 1318

View of frankpledge in the same place, the day and year abovesaid

Common fine 5s. 1d.	All the chief pledges give as the common fine 5s. 1d.
All the chief pledges Amercement 3d.	present that William Heynon has made an encroachment by digging up the ground in a certain lane which leads from the house of John the cook towards Chatham green, therefore he is in mercy, on the surety of John Cook and John Lytle.
Amercement 3d.	Also they present that William Mot has made an encroachment by putting dung in the common street to the annoyance of the lord and of the neighbours, therefore he is in mercy.
Amercement 6d.	Also they present that Robert Leuelif has made an encroachment with one wall by stopping up a certain course of water to the annoyance of the neighbours, therefore he is in mercy, on the surety of John Cok and William Heynon, and order is made to remove the said wall.
Fine 2s.	And afterwards the said Robert made a fine that the said wall might stand in peace because it does not stand to great annoyance, on the surety of the said John Cook and William Heynon.
Amercement 3d.	Also they present that Robert Leuelif has made an encroachment by putting dung in the common street to the annoyance of the neighbours, therefore he is in mercy, on the surety of John Cok and William Heynon.
Amercement 2d. Order made	Also they present that Thomas Randolf has made an encroachment with a certain hedge by Colkeslane to the annoyance of James of La Hyde and others, therefore he is in mercy, on the surety of Adam Rat and Richard Hwytbred, and order is made to remove the said encroachment.
Order made	Also they present that the Lord ought to cleanse the ditch by the lane below his Courthouse, by which the neighbouring way in wintertime is completely submerged to the annoyance of the neighbours.
Amercement 3d.	Also they present that Richard, son of Richard Hwytbred, has made default, therefore he is in mercy.

*See p.*22.

Extract from Manorial Survey, Thaxted, *c.*1395

Thomas Tewe holds 6 acres of pasture and does common suit and pays annually				1d.
The same John Benge holds one grove, lately of Roger atte Welde and pays annually		1½d.		1½d.
William Yerdele holds one messuage and one acre of land	4d.	4d.	4d.	4d.
John Proude holds 4 acres of land out of the tenement James, which tenement owes common suit and pays annually	4d.	4d.	4d.	4d.
Henry Boyton holds one messuage and 30 acres of land, meadow and pasture, and owes common suit and pays		15s.		15s.
The same Henry holds a half-virgate of land out of the tenement once Golsmyth, and owes common suit and does 3 carriages of corn and hay recovering from the lord 4½d. or he shall give to the lord 6d., and pays annually	20¼d.	20¼d.	20¼d.	20¼d.
William Symond holds 3 acres of land and pays annually	4½d. 1 capon	4½d.	4½d.	4½d.
Thomas May holds 6 acres of land and one purpresture and pays	4¼d.	4¼d.	4¼d.	4¼d.
Walter Ewayn holds 6 acres of land and 1 piece of meadow and pays	2¼d.	2¼d.	2¼d.	2¼d.
John Herry, butcher, holds 1 acre of land and pays	1d.	1d.	1d.	1d
John Thrower, John Dod, hold one acre of land and pay annually	1d.	1d.	1d.	1d

*See p.*23.

SHORT LIST OF BOOKS FOR DETAILED STUDY AND REFERENCE

Thompson, Sir E. M.: *Introduction to Greek and Latin Palaeography* (1912). Includes facsimiles and transcripts.

Johnson, C., and Jenkinson, H.: *English Court Hand, A.D. 1066 to 1500* (1915). Includes sections on evolution of court hand, writing materials, methods of abbreviation, common abbreviations; illustrates forms of individual letters, special signs, numerals, punctuation, etc., at different dates. Facsimiles and transcripts. Bibliography.

Jenkinson, H.: *The Later Court Hands in England, from the 15th to the 17th century* (1927). Includes illustrated sections on different hands, methods of abbreviation and special signs, numerals, punctuation, etc. Writing Masters' alphabets, facsimiles and transcripts. Bibliography.

Greg, W. W.: *English Literary Autographs, 1550-1650* (1925-32). Facsimiles, transcripts and notes.

Judge, C. B.: *Specimens of Sixteenth Century English Handwriting* (1935). Notes on methods of abbreviation. Writing Masters' alphabets and facsimiles but no transcripts. Bibliography.

Grieve, H. E. P.: *Some Examples of English Handwriting* (1949). Facsimiles and transcripts from Essex official, ecclesiastical, estate and family archives of the 12th to the 17th century.

Denholm-Young, N.: *Handwriting in England and Wales* (1954). Includes facsimiles and a few transcripts.

Hector, L. C.: *The Handwriting of English Documents* (1958). Includes facsimiles and transcripts.

Heal, A.: *The English Writing Masters and their Copy-books, 1570-1800* (1931). Introduction on scripts by Stanley Morison.

Schulz, H. C.: 'The Teaching of Handwriting in Tudor and Stuart Times', in *Huntington Library Quarterly*, VI (1943), 381-425.

Tschichold, J.: *An Illustrated History of Writing and Lettering* (1947).

Fairbank, A.: *A Book of Scripts* (King Penguin, 1949).

Martin, C. T.: *The Record Interpreter* (2nd edn. 1910). Abbreviations; glossary of Latin words; Latin forms of names.

Lindsay, W. M.: *Notae Latinae* (1915). An account of abbreviation in Latin MSS. of the early minuscule period, *c.*700-850.

Bains, D.: *A Supplement to Notae Latinae* (1936). Abbreviations in Latin MSS. of 850 to 1050 A.D.

Baxter, J. H., and Johnson, C.: *Medieval Latin Word-List* (1934).

Cappelli, A.: *Dizionario di Abbreviature Latine ed Italiane* (4th edn. 1949). Abbreviations

Powicke, F. M. (Editor): *Handbook of British Chronology* (1939).

Cheney, C. R. (Editor): *Handbook of Dates for Students of English History* (1948).

Report on editing historical documents, in *Bulletin of the Institute of Historical Research*, vol. i (1923). Rules for making an accurate transcript.

British Records Association: *Notes for the Guidance of Editors of Record Publications* (1946). Rules for transcribing.

In addition, for most areas there are books to help with purely local difficulties, such as place and field-names, dialect words, etc.